GROUP COUNSELING
FOR SECONDARY SCHOOLS

ABOUT THE AUTHOR

Dorothy J. Scrivner Blum received the Virginia Counselor of the Year Award of 1988 and the Virginia Secondary School Counselor of the Year Award of 1984. She is a Licensed Professional Counselor (LPC) in the Commonwealth of Virginia and a National Certified Counselor (NCC). Her doctorate degree is in Counselor Education from the University of Virginia. Her other degrees are from the University of Nebraska (M.M.) and Midland College (A.B.)

Dorothy Blum was the guidance director at George C. Marshall High School in Fairfax County Public Schools, Falls Church, Virginia for ten years and currently she is the Coordinator of Elementary Guidance in Fairfax County Public Schools. She was a school counselor in La Canada Junior High School and La Canada Senior High School in California.

This author has taught the graduate course, "Group Counseling Procedures," for the University of Virginia in Charlottesville, Henrico County and Fairfax County; for Western Maryland College, in Westminster and Frederick County Maryland; and for Virginia Polytechnic Institute and University, in Fairfax County Virginia.

GROUP COUNSELING FOR SECONDARY SCHOOLS

By

DOROTHY J. SCRIVNER BLUM (ED.), ED.D., LPC, NCC

And Contributing School Counselors

Fairfax County Public Schools
Virginia Polytechnic Institute and University
Education Department

CHARLES C THOMAS • PUBLISHER
Springfield • Illinois • U.S.A.

Published and Distributed Throughout the World by
CHARLES C THOMAS • PUBLISHER
2600 South First Street
Springfield, Illinois 62794-9265

This book is protected by copyright. No part of
it may be reproduced in any manner without
written permission from the publisher.

© *1990 by* CHARLES C THOMAS • PUBLISHER

ISBN 0-398-05637-4

Library of Congress Catalog Card Number: 89-39300

With THOMAS BOOKS *careful attention is given to all details of manufacturing and design. It is the Publisher's desire to present books that are satisfactory as to their physical qualities and artistic possibilities and appropriate for their particular use.* THOMAS BOOKS *will be true to those laws of quality that assure a good name and good will.*

Printed in the United States of America
SC-R-3

Library of Congress Cataloging-in-Publication Data

Group counseling for secondary schools / by Dorothy J. Scrivner Blum
 (ad.), and contributing school counselors.
   p.   cm.
  Includes bibliographical references.
  ISBN 0-398-05637-4
  1. Personnel service in secondary education. 2. Group guidance in
education. 3. Peer counseling of students.   I. Blum, Dorothy.
LB1620.4.G76   1989
373.14—dc20   89-39300
                                                                           CIP

CONTRIBUTORS

Aldridge, Marcella: B.S., University of Florida, Gainesville, FL; M. Ed. Guidance from Virginia Polytechnic Institute and University (VPI), Blacksburg, VA. Counselor for two years in the Administration Office, Columbia Public Schools, Columbia, SC; Counselor for two years for Student Services, Department of Defense, Far East; and Counselor for four years at Chantilly High School, Chantilly, VA, Fairfax County Public Schools (FCPS).

Calbert, Thelma: B.S., Jackson State University, Jackson, MS; M.Ed. Guidance and Counseling from University of Illinois, Urbana, IL. Counselor for one year at Rowan Junior High School, Jackson, MS; Counselor for two years at Lawrence High School, Lawrence, KS; Coordinator of Freshman Services for one year at Alabama State University, Montgomery, AL; and Counselor for seventeen years at Herndon High School, Herndon, VA, FCPS.

Carmichael, Elyse: B.S., University of Georgia, Athens, GA; M.Ed. Counseling from University of Virginia, Charlottesville, VA. Counselor for three years at Burley Middle School, Charlottesville, VA, Albemarle County Public Schools; Counselor for five years at George C. Marshall High School, Falls Church, VA, FCPS.

Carroll, Marguerite: Ph.D., Professor, Counselor Education for the University of Southern Maine. Previous Professor of Counselor Education at Fairfield, University. Fellow, Association for Specialists in Group Work. Past President of the Association for Specialists in Group Work.

Francis, Anita: B.A., Reed College, Portland, OR; M.Ed. Guidance and Counseling from George Mason University, Fairfax, VA. Counselor for ten years at Langley High School, McLean, VA, FCPS. Counselor for one year at Stuart High School, Falls Church, VA, FCPS.

Gaudreault, Ken: B.S. from Tennessee Technical University, Cookeville, TE; M.A. in School Administration from Northern Colorado University,

Greeley, CO; Certified in Guidance from VPI. Counselor for seven years at Mount Vernon High School, Alexandria, VA, FCPS; Guidance Director for one year at Sandburg Intermediate School, Alexandria, FCPS.

Holman, Celestine: B.S. from Florida Agricultural and Mechanical (A & M) University, Tallahassee, FL; M.Ed. Guidance from Alabama A & M, Normal, AL. Counselor for one year at the University of Alabama, Huntsville, AL; Career Counselor for two years for the Department of Defense in Germany; Counselor for six years at Stuart High School, Falls Church, VA; and Counselor for five years at West Springfield High School, Springfield, VA, FCPS.

Lunter, Margaret: A.B. from Glenville State College, Glenville, WV; M.A. Guidance from Marshall University, Huntington, WV. Counselor for eight years at Mount Vernon High School, Alexandria, VA, FCPS; Counselor for one year at Thomas Jefferson School for Science and Technology, Alexandria, VA, FCPS.

McCann, Barbara: B.S., University of Wisconsin, Madison, WI; M.A. in Educational Counseling from California State University at San Jose, CA. Counselor/Teacher for one year at San Jose Unified School District, CA; Counselor for two years in Dryden Elementary School, Dryden, NY; and Counselor for eleven years at Marshall High School, Falls Church, VA, FCPS.

Perlstein, Ruth: B.A., Douglas College, New Brunswick, NJ; M.Ed. Counseling and Guidance from Rutgers State University, New Brunswick, NJ. Counselor for two years at Woodstowne High School, Woodstowne, NJ; Counselor for two years at Greenfield High School, Milwaukee, WI; Counselor for one year at Hammond High School, Alexandria, VA, Alexandria City Public Schools; Counselor for thirteen years at Groveton High School, Alexandria, VA, FCPS; Teacher/Consultant for one year for the Northern Virginia Writers' Project, George Mason University, Fairfax, VA; Counselor for four years at West Potomac High School, Alexandria, VA, FCPS.

Riddick, Georgia: B.S., Virginia State University, Petersburg, VA; M.Ed. Counselor Education from Boston University, Boston, MA. Counselor for four years at Robinson Secondary School, Fairfax, VA, FCPS; Counselor for two years at Marshall High School, Falls Church, VA; Counselor for one year at Mount Vernon High School, Alexandria, VA, FCPS.

Saslaw, Eleanor B.: B.A., University of Maryland, College Park, MD;

M.A. Secondary School Counseling from University of Maryland. Counselor for one year at Herndon High School, Herndon, VA; Counselor for ten years at Annandale High School, Annandale, VA, FCPS; Counselor for three years at Thomas Jefferson School of Science and Technology, Alexandria, VA, FCPS.

*This book is dedicated to Richard G. Blum
for his enduring patience and encouragement.*

FOREWORD

MARGUERITE (PEG) CARROLL, PH.D., NCC
PROFESSOR EMERITUS, FAIRFIELD UNIVERSITY

The concept of group work has long been seen as a panacea for school counselors because through this process counselors could have the greatest influence on the most number of students. The irony however, has been that the school itself, its organizational systems and its priorities, has been the very obstacle denying the actual implementation of group counseling as a learning process within the school.

This book makes a significant contribution to the evolution of this issue because it provides the secondary school counselor with a way to implement processes in group work which are at the heart of issues deeply rooted in the school. These topics are related to such issues as the ongoing responsibility for developing effective social skills, relieving stress, developing values, abuse of alcohol, facing family problems, and dealing with test anxiety, to name but a few areas addressed. These issues are central to the climate of school life today.

Dorothy Blum, the editor of this creative work, has spent most of her professional life working with young people. The chapters are written by various authors under Dorothy Blum's direction and supervision. The topics addressed indicate that Dorothy and her writers are at the zenith of the idiosyncratic issues of the day.

Texts about group work usually include lengthy discussion devoted to group rationale, group theory, group goal setting, and of course these publications have significant value in the counselor's library. This volume however, goes beyond fundamental background material to meet a direct need of the counselor in the school. It is timely, it is pragmatic and practical. In the most positive fashion the counselor is taken through a step by step process of group work while topics and social issues are developed through the medium of group counseling. The process described helps students value their discoveries and become participants in the common search for solving problems which overwhelm them. Through each topic addressed, the counselor is given a road map to help young people develop a sense of their individual and collective strength.

The secondary school counselor will come to the close of this book convinced of the necessity to address these topics and issues with young people. Each author presents a recurring view of the same process. Each time the process is seen from a slightly different angle, until suddenly the reader has recognized some wider truth about the meaning and importance of group counseling. Group counseling is presented as a learning and growing process which can make a significant contribution to the unfolding lives of young people.

PREFACE

School counselors are busy counseling students, consulting with parents, teachers, and administrators, arranging and changing schedules, providing information about colleges and financial aid, administering and interpreting standardized tests, and attempting to prevent substance abuse, drop-outs, and suicides. They do not have time to plan for group counseling, even though they recognize the value of well-planned groups with specified goals and skilled leaders.

In a national survey on the status of secondary school guidance, Peer (1985) surveyed fifty state guidance directors. He found that 62 percent of the thirty-seven respondents "doubted that secondary school programs were actively involved in providing group counseling services" (p. 184). As a result, Bowman (1987) designed and conducted a study to learn the reason so few high school counselors provide group counseling. He concluded that "more small-group 'how to' strategies are needed." He stated:

> Small-group guidance and counseling has been held in high regard by the counseling profession for decades. It is a tool that counselors can use more effectively and efficiently than other approaches to make some gains with students. Now is the time to develop, study, and share more specific strategies to assist the practicing counselor in implementing and using this powerful tool with more confidence (Bowman, 1987, p. 261).

The plans in this book are "how to" strategies written by school counselors for school counselors. Each session can be completed within one period of fifty minutes, and the activities are appropriate for students at specific grade levels. The group procedures are planned to achieve particular goals.

These group proposals are written according to a particular format. The rationale provides the reason that the counselor believes that this plan fulfills a need in the school; the goals for the group are realistic and measurable; the definition of the group indicates the number of members, and the duration and frequency of the sessions. The procedures address, and logically will achieve the goals. The evaluation instrument is practical and measures the members' perceptions of the achievement of the specified goals and the procedures.

REFERENCES

Blum, Dorothy J.: Group leadership training: An inclusive model. *Journal for Specialists in Group Work.* 8(2);76–85, May 1983.

Bowman, Robert P.: Small-group guidance and counseling in schools: A national survey of school counselors. *The School Counselor.* 34(4):256–262, March 1987.

Peer, Gary G.: The status of secondary school guidance: A national survey. *The School Counselor.* 32(3):181–189, January 1985.

ACKNOWLEDGEMENT

This collection of proposals for groups in schools is the result of the encouragement of group counseling in the Fairfax County Public Schools; the provision of practical graduate courses by Virginia Tech, Falls Church Center; and the promotion of group counseling as a worthy project by Charles C Thomas, Publisher.

INTRODUCTION

GUIDELINES FOR A SUCCESSFUL GROUP COUNSELING PROGRAM

The proposals for groups in this publication were designed based upon specific assumptions about group counseling in schools that should be made explicit.

1. Everyone can benefit from group counseling. Too often groups have been conducted only for students with apparent problems. A good group counseling program addresses many student needs and students *want* to join. Students, teachers, parents and administrators see positive results when students are involved in a good group counseling program.
2. School time is very precious, concrete and limited. When a student is excused from class to attend group counseling, the leader is responsible for having a plan to logically bring about specific goals. The leader must use group counseling time judiciously.
3. Each session should lead toward achieving stated objectives and goals. Procedures should be planned and written so that experiences in group counseling logically result in achievement of stated goals and skills used throughout life.
4. When students experience problems in their lives they do not learn readily or easily. If they can discuss these problems and "work them out" in a group led by a qualified and trained counselor, they are more ready to learn. When group members have strong feelings of anger, distress, sadness, or when something has happened to them during the week that has an intense effect on them, they are invited to share these with the group. Expressing intense feelings or important events of the week has precedence over following the plan for the group session when the leader believes all members are learning from the experience. When the value of

the members' learning is questionable, the leader must intervene and return to the plan for the group session.
5. Administrative support is crucial for a group counseling program. Counselors can show the written plan for a specific group to the administrator before leading the group so the administrator is informed and can justify the reason that students are excused from class to attend group sessions. After the group, with group members' permission, anonymous written evaluations of the group experience may be shared with the administrator. Favorable evaluations bring about vital administrative support and result in a strong group counseling program.
6. Individual screening interviews with interested potential members must be conducted by the leader before the first group session if the counselor who is leading the group does not already know the students. Questions to ask during this interview are specified.
7. Membership in groups should be voluntary. Members should not be put in a group as a disciplinary measure. Students may refer themselves, or they may be referred by their parent, teacher, administrator, counselor or even friends. Although the students may be referred by others, the prospective members should want to be in the group. The final selection of members should be determined by the leader(s) who is/are aware of the need for positive peer role models in each group.
8. Confidentiality promotes trust and protects members so their concerns are not discussed indiscriminately with people outside the group. Sometimes group members find it helpful to discuss their own goal and progress outside the group. The degree of confidentiality should be discussed and agreed upon by all members at the first session of the group. When a member reveals particularly sensitive information during a group session, the leader reminds members of their pledge and agreement for confidentiality. During the last meeting of the group the leader again reminds the members of their responsibility to keep in confidence what was said by others in the group sessions.
9. The quarter and semester school structure makes it logical that groups meet for one quarter (eight or nine weekly sessions) and each session lasts one period (approximately fifty minutes). A rotating schedule of group sessions permits members to meet

weekly for a quarter without missing one class more than one or two times. There may be exceptions.
10. Teachers are cooperative with the group program if they know in advance the dates and periods students will be absent. The leader should inform prospective members that class assignments must be completed and handed in before attending group. Furthermore, teachers are assured that group members are to take tests with the rest of the class and are excused from the group when they have tests.
11. When school systems require written parental permission for students involved in group counseling, the leader obtains this written permission before students are admitted to any group sessions.
12. Members should evaluate the group experience anonymously, objectively, and in writing. The evaluation instrument should measure the achievement of the stated group goals as well as the procedures used in the group. With members' permission, their teachers and/or parents also may be asked to measure the students' progress.
13. A positive group counseling program results when the following model is followed:
    a. Determine the need for a specific group.
    b. Design a plan for the specific group based upon the determined need.
    c. Determine and state specific goals for members to achieve as a result of the group experience.
    d. Plan procedures to logically achieve the stated goals.
    e. Evaluate the achievement of the goals and the procedures used to achieve the goals.
    f. Revise the plan to design a more effective group next time. Everything can improve!

CONTENTS

	Page
Foreword	xi
Preface	xiii
Introduction	xvii

Chapter One
IMPROVE ACADEMIC PERFORMANCE
Improve Grades in High School — *Margaret Lunter* 3

Chapter Two
COUNSEL THE GIFTED
Perfectionism of Gifted High School Students — *Eleanor Saslaw* 23

Chapter Three
DEAL POSITIVELY WITH STRESS
Test-Anxiety — *Celestine N. Holman* 41

Chapter Four
HELP NEWCOMERS
Newcomers' Seminar — *Anita Francis* 55

Chapter Five
HELP TEENAGERS OF CHANGING FAMILIES
Seminar for Adolescents Living with Parents Who are Separated or Divorced — *Marcella C. Aldridge* 65

Chapter Six
WRITE FOR SELF-UNDERSTANDING
Write a College Application Essay — *Ruth Perlstein* 79

Chapter Seven
INCREASE CAREER AWARENESS
Career Awareness for High School Freshmen — *Kenneth A. Gaudreault* ... 95

Chapter Eight
DEVELOP INDIVIDUAL POTENTIAL
Individual Student Growth
through Group Counseling—*Barbara McCann*................... 115

Chapter Nine
DEVELOP POSITIVE HUMAN RELATIONS AMONG ETHNIC GROUPS
Getting to Know You:
Race Relations is Everybody's Responsibility—*Georgia G. Riddick*... 123

Chapter Ten
LEARN TO HELP OTHERS
Preparing Peer Counselors
to Work With Younger Students—*Elyse Carmichael*................ 141

Chapter Eleven
PREVENT SUBSTANCE ABUSE
Help Students Stay Sober—*Dorothy J. Scrivner Blum*................ 149

Chapter Twelve
PREVENT DROPOUTS
Who Am I?—*Thelma Nichols Calbert*........................ 157
Index.. 171

GROUP COUNSELING FOR SECONDARY SCHOOLS

Chapter One

IMPROVE ACADEMIC PERFORMANCE

Proposal One

IMPROVE GRADES IN HIGH SCHOOL

Margaret Lunter

Rationale

Most adolescents are concerned about their report card grades. They may only want Mom or Dad to quit nagging, but these students express a desire to improve their school work. Other students appear to have no concern over their failing grades, but actually they too, wish to be more successful in school. Students who do not do well academically frequently are unable to communicate the frustration they feel. They do not know how to seek help, and consequently they withdraw or resort to distracting behavior. These students' communication skills are so limited that they are unable to take steps toward succeeding in school.

After getting the students' first report cards of the year, parents frequently request weekly progress reports of students' grades from teachers, hoping to receive evidence of improvement. Students also desire to take home acceptable reports. Distributing, monitoring, and following-up with progress reports is a time-consuming and difficult task for the counselor and progress reports are not effective in helping students learn, achieve academically, or improve their grades.

This seminar, designed to help freshmen improve their grades, is a direct result of student interest. Participants set their own individual goals indicating how much they believe they can improve their grades.

Goals

Students are expected to achieve four primary goals as a result of this seminar:

1. Develop and use effective communication skills.
2. Learn and demonstrate specific techniques to improve study habits.
3. Establish and use a method to monitor individual progress.
4. Work together in the group to help each other improve grades.

Membership

The group consists of ten to twelve ninth grade students who have expressed an interest in improving their grades. Males, females and minority students are included. Two or three students who have average or above average grades are role models in the group. By participating in this seminar they are motivated to continue to improve their academic performance.

Publicizing This Seminar

Students whose parents have requested weekly progress reports are given an opportunity to participate, but the *students* must *want* to be members of the group.

Information about this seminar is posted on the door to the guidance office (Appendix 1-1). Notices are printed in the student bulletin and the Parent and Teacher Association (PTA) newsletter, explaining the purpose and goals of this seminar.

Meetings

Meetings are held weekly, alternating the periods each week. Homework is to be handed in to the teacher prior to attending group sessions and students are excused from the group when they have tests. The schedule of group meetings is provided to the teachers (Appendix 1-3).

Screening Interview

Interested students are screened individually by the counselor using guidelines (Appendix 1-5). After the counselor interviews interested students and selects twelve to participate, he/she gives the selected participants a letter for parental permission (Appendix 1-2). The teachers are given a written explanation of the seminar (Appendix 1-3) and a schedule of the sessions (Appendix 1-4). Candidates who are not selected are provided options to improve their grades, such as using the teacher's help after school or using the tutoring service.

Outline of the Sessions

Session 1

Objective: Help each member set his/her personal goal for the seminar.
Energizer: "Expanded Name Tag"

Give each member a five inch circle of colored construction paper and a felt tip pen. Read the following directions aloud:

1. Write your name in the center of the circle.
2. At the top of the circle write your birthplace.
3. On the left side of the circle write your favorite place.
4. On the right side of the circle write your favorite activity.
5. At the bottom write the name of the thing or situation you dislike most.
6. Find a partner in the group and talk with him/her about his/her name tag for two minutes.
7. Introduce your partner to the group.

Content: Distribute pencils and folders with paper and cards. Explain that members may decorate their folders any way they would like, to identify them without their names.

Review the meeting schedule and ask students to keep copies of it in their folders. Ask group members to remind their teachers each day before the seminar, that they will be absent from class the following day. If there is an assignment, the member can discuss it with the teacher at that time.

Explain the ground rules for the meetings (Appendix 1-6) and post them in the meeting room.

Introduce goal setting by telling them that the purpose of this group is to help them deal with a problem they all have in common. They all have said that they want to improve their grades.

Ask them to write on the bottom inside pocket of their folders, the specific improvement they want to strive for. They are to be specific and realistic. They should indicate the course or courses they will concentrate on and the grade(s) they will work for. "Will you choose one course or several?" "Do you want to raise all your quarter grades to a C or better?" "Will you try to raise each of your grades one letter?" "Is your goal to make the honor roll?"

After members have had time to consider and write their goals, ask volunteers to read them. As each person reads his/her goal, ask the group to determine if the goal meets the criteria for goal setting (Appendix 1-7).

Ask students to write the specific barriers that could keep them from reaching their goals on a card. Then invite volunteers to talk about the barriers they have identified, and list them on a sheet of newsprint. Discuss how to overcome these barriers.

Closure: Using the card included in the pocket of the folder, each member writes a response: "Today I learned...." (Appendix 1-8)

Session 2

Objective: Identify resources which will help students meet their personal goals.

Energizer: "Connect the Dots." Ask members to connect the nine dots without lifting their pencil (Appendix 1-9, Illustration 1-1). The exercise shows that sometimes we must "go outside the expected" to meet our goal.

Discuss what it means to "go outside" to meet the goal of improving grades. It means asking a teacher, parents or another student for help, using the library, or using an allowance to buy school supplies such as a dictionary, a thesaurus, pencils, pens, paper, or notebooks.

Content: Review each student's individual goals. Discuss the steps that must be followed to meet the established goals:

1. Set aside specific time to complete homework.
2. Know what the teacher expects of students in the course, the specific assignment each day, and the grading policy of the teacher. Discuss the importance of knowing what is expected.
3. Ask the teacher for information or help. Demonstrate how to respectfully ask a teacher for help.

Assignment for Next Session: For each class in which the members want to improve, they are to bring an outline of the quarter requirements for that course, and prepare an explanation of the grading policy.

Session 3

Objective: Help students use problem-solving techniques to meet their personal goals.
Content: Introduce problem solving by giving examples of the ways people solve problems: by impulse, procrastination, not deciding, or by letting others decide. Ask how students currently solve problems. Evaluate all the methods and then provide the steps for problem solving (Appendix 1-10).

Divide the group into dyads. Each person tells his/her partner the requirements and the grading policy for the course he/she selected. The dyad partners develop techniques to meet each member's goal in that course. After fifteen minutes in the dyad, the entire group reassembles and the members of each dyad present to the entire group, the problem, the alternatives discussed, and the steps to follow for solution. The members ask questions and make suggestions, but the member who set the goal selects the steps to achieve it.
Closure: Ask members to complete the statement in Appendix 1-8.

Session 4

Objective: Help students determine their personal learning style.
Materials: Copies of "How I Process Information" and "Satisfying Learning Experiences" (Appendices 1-11 and 1-12).
Energizer: "Way Out." Ask members to stand and join hands in a circle. Release the hand of the member on your left; then lead the line, weaving your way through the group, going under their joined hands. Members follow without letting go of hands. After weaving through the group, stop and tell the group that now the members must get back into the circle without letting go of hands.
Content: Explain that there are different styles of learning and stress that one is not better than another. Suggest that students may learn their style of learning by selecting their answers to the items in "How I Process Information" (Appendix 1-11). Then read how their different answers reflect their preferred learning styles. Lead a discussion of the members' preferred learning styles to find out if this pattern is consistent with other learning in their lives. Look for differences among the group.

Distribute cards, the directions, and worksheet for "Satisfying Learning Experiences" (Appendix 1-12). Ask students to follow the directions and complete the worksheet to learn if these answers are consistent with the previous activity.

Discuss the things they learned about themselves from these two activities. Focus on ways school work can be completed using their most satisfying learning style.

Closure: Ask members to complete the statement in Appendix 1-8.

Session 5

Objective: Help students establish a routine for productive study habits.
Energizer: "Four Corners." In each of the four corners of the room, place a poster with one letter, A, B, C, or D. Give the following directions: "Listen to the questions I ask. There is a letter posted in each corner of the room. Choose the letter which indicates your answer to the question, and then go to that corner."

1. How do you react when you are asked a question in class and you don't know the answer? A. Fake it; B. Say you don't know; C. Act ashamed; D. Laugh.
2. How do you feel when someone else is unjustly punished? A. Silently angry; B. Calm, unconcerned; C. Confused; D. As if you should tell the punisher that he/she is wrong.
3. How do you feel about being corrected by the teacher? A. Angry; B. Grateful; C. Embarrassed; D. Threatened.
4. How do you feel about being corrected by peers? A. Stupid; B. Disliked; C. Pleased; D. Hurt.
5. How do you feel toward a teacher's pet? A. Jealous; B. Admiring; C. Indifferent; D. Antagonistic.
6. How does a permissive teacher make you feel? A. Happy; B. Insecure; C. Cheated, disappointed; D. Puzzled.
7. What is your attitude toward a friend who has wronged you? A. Extremely angry; B. Hurt; C. Revengeful; D. Not caring.
8. How do you feel when you see someone cheating on a difficult test that you studied hard for: A. Extremely angry; B. Hurt; C. Revengeful; D. Not caring.

Reassemble the group and lead a discussion as the students give their reasons for selecting their answers.
Content: Discuss four essentials to good health: (1) recreation; (2) sleep; (3) exercise; (4) nutrition.

Ask students to write their answers to these questions on a card.

1. The best place for me to study is. . . .
2. The best time for me to study is. . . .
3. The best length of time for me to study is. . . .

Discuss differences and similarities in answers. Talk about these as being productive study techniques. Suggest that members write a personal schedule for a day including time for study, recreation, sleep, exercise and eating. If this works well, then recommend that they follow the schedule for a week and then a month. Ask students to write a schedule and try to follow it and report the success to the group the next session.

Closure: Ask members to complete the statement in Appendix 1-8.

Session 6

Objective: Introduce effective communication skills.
Energizer: "Communication Exercise." Designs for this activity are in Napier & Gershenfeld, 1973.

Ask a volunteer to sit with his/her back to the group. Show the group a complex design that members are to describe to the volunteer who has not seen the design. The volunteer tries to draw the design from the description provided by the group. Only one-way communication is allowed. The volunteer *cannot* ask any questions. Ask the volunteer to share his/her frustration at not being able to ask questions.

Repeat the activity, showing the group an even more complex design to describe, but this time the volunteer can ask questions and the group can answer the questions. Lead a discussion about how it is easier to understand directions and information when there is two-way communication.

Content: After giving members the unfinished sentences below, ask them to listen and then repeat each other's endings to these unfinished sentences. Members of the group will respond in turn:

1. If I had my own car. . . .
2. I feel best when people. . . .
3. If I had a million dollars I would. . . .
4. Secretly I wish. . . .

The purpose for this activity is to encourage students to listen to and trust each other. Discuss as appropriate.

Review personal schedules written last session. Help each member to assess his/her own desire and ability to follow the schedule.

Review the "I Learned" statements as a review of this session.

Session 7

Objective: Help students practice effective communication skills.

Energizer: "Magic Box." Say to the group: "In front of you is a box. If this box could deliver to you the one thing that would make you happy, what would be in the box?" Students write their responses on an unsigned card. If any student does not want others to know what he/she wrote, that member may keep his/her card. Collect the cards of the risk takers and read them aloud to the group, as members try to guess the authors.

Content: Lead a discussion about how people inhibit communication. Provide the list of roadblocks to effective communication. Ask members to make statements which are examples of each and discuss.

- Arguing
- Judging
- Criticizing
- Blaming
- Ridiculing
- Sarcasm
- Persuading
- Presenting facts

Discuss techniques to facilitate communication:

- Use eye contact.
- Face the person you are talking to.
- Allow one person to speak at a time.
- Use "I Messages." Describe an "I Message" (see Chapter Eight, Proposal one) and give examples.
- Listen carefully to what others say.

Volunteers demonstrate effective communication skills by responding appropriately to the following:

1. The homework for tomorrow's English class will take an hour to complete. You already have another commitment for the evening and you don't know how you will be able to complete the assignment. The teacher has just assigned the homework today and he/she

said that if anyone has a problem with the assignment to let him/her know.
2. Your algebra test grade is $D+$ but when you compute it, you get a C. Your counselor and your mother have suggested that you go to the teacher to discuss it.
3. Today you were late to French class because you stopped to help another teacher carry some books. This is your third tardy to French. Your French teacher has assigned you a one hour detention for being late to class.
4. You asked for help in science and the teacher ignored you.
5. You came after school for an appointment with the teacher, but the teacher was not there.
6. You didn't get to write down all the details of the history assignment because the teacher talked too fast or erased the board too fast.

Discuss the effectiveness of each response in terms of honesty of the student and feelings of the teacher. If members have any problems similar to those demonstrated, suggest that they practice their communication with the group first, and then use the skill when talking with their teacher. Ask them to report back to the group about the effectiveness of their talk with the teacher.

Session 8

Objective: Introduce effective listening and responding skills.
Energizer: "I Got Rhythm." This activity reinforces good listening and responding skills.
Participants sit in a circle. Begin the rhythm, hitting thighs twice, then clapping twice, and saying "I got rhy-thm," to the beat. On the second sequence, call your own name as you clap. On the third sequence, call another member's name as you clap your hands. That member continues the rhythm, giving his/her own name during the first sequence, and names another person in the circle as he/she claps his/ her hands in the second sequence. The rhythm continues until it is broken by someone who misses the beat without a name.
Content: Ask the results of the members who were going to talk with their teacher. Ask if other members experienced any reasons to have

meetings with their teachers. If so, suggest that they describe and then role play the situation for practice and help before going to the teacher.

Discuss possible noise distractions that may interfere with effective listening:

1. Outside noise (in the hall, street, other people talking, stereo or TV playing).
2. Inside noise (something in the room like a pet, a fan, the furnace, stereo, chair squeak.)
3. Self-talk (thinking about how we look, thinking we may sound stupid, daydreaming.)

Listening Skills Exercise: Use a tape recorder. Ask a volunteer to read a few sentences and have another volunteer repeat the sentences verbatim. Play the tape to check on accuracy. Divide participants into dyads. One person speaks a ten to fifteen word sentence and the other person, after a brief pause, repeats the sentence verbatim. This exercise should be repeated several times by each partner to highlight the ability of each partner to listen effectively. Discuss "noise" that might have prevented effective listening.

Assignment for Final Session: "Arrange a private conference with the teacher in whose class/es you are working for improvement. Ask for your nine week evaluation and bring the information to the final session. Try to remember exactly what the teacher says. You may take notes."

Closure: Ask members to complete the statement in Appendix 1-8.

Session 9

Objective: Summarize the skills the members learned in this seminar, and ask members to assess their success in reaching the goal they set at the beginning of the seminar.

Content: Ask members to review their personal goal and report on the progress they have made toward reaching it. Members provide information they received during their conference with their teacher(s). If warranted, praise the student, if not, solicit suggestions from the group as to how the member can make progress.

Closure: Bring closure to the group with the activity "Hope Chest" (Appendix 1-13).

Ask members to complete the evaluation form (Appendix 1-14).

Follow-Up Session

Write an invitation to each member to attend the follow-up session, and if they wish they may invite their parents or teachers as guests. With the members' permission, you may also invite the principal and counselors of the members. If you wish to give certificates of completion, they could be distributed during this session.

An alternative is a session that only includes the members, and they are invited to bring their pre-session report card and their post-session report card to compare and share.

Appendix 1-1

POSTER ON GUIDANCE BULLETIN BOARD OR DOOR

(In large print, not typed)

ARE YOUR GRADES LOWER THAN YOU WANT THEM TO BE?

DO YOU SECRETLY WISH YOU WERE ON THE HONOR ROLL?

ARE YOU A *"C"* STUDENT WHO WOULD LIKE TO BE A *"B"* STUDENT?

WOULD YOU LIKE TO LEARN *HOW TO IMPROVE YOUR GRADES?*

TELL MR./MS. _____ YOU ARE INTERESTED IN THE SEMINAR HE/SHE IS LEADING THIS QUARTER. STUDENTS WHO PARTICIPATE WILL LEARN TO SET GOALS, COMMUNICATE EFFECTIVELY, AND PRACTICE EFFECTIVE PROBLEM SOLVING. THEY ALSO WILL FIND OUT ABOUT THEIR LEARNING STYLE. ONLY STUDENTS WHO REALLY WANT TO BE A PART OF THIS SEMINAR WILL BE SELECTED.

Appendix 1-2

LETTER TO PARENTS

Date

Dear Parent,

_____ has expressed an interest in participating in a group/seminar entitled _____. The goal for this group/seminar is to help students _____.

_____ weekly sessions are planned, meeting during a different period each week so the members miss a minimum amount of instruction from each class. Members are responsible for work missed from class.

I am the leader of this group/seminar and the first meeting is _____. I believe your son/daughter will benefit from this group experience.

Members need parental permission to participate. If you have any questions before signing the permission form, please call me at _____ - _____. I look forward to meeting with this group.

Sincerely,

- -

_____ has my permission to participate in the _____ group/seminar described above.

_____   _____
         Date   Parent Signature

Appendix 1-3

TEACHER NOTIFICATION

DATE: _____
TO: _____
FROM: _____, Counselor
RE.: _____ Group Counseling Seminar

_____ has parent permission and will be participating in a group seminar from _____ to _____. The rotating schedule of meetings is attached.

This student is responsible for making up work missed and will remind you in advance of the particular day he/she will miss your class. Members are excused from group the day of a scheduled test. Please let me know if this student is in danger of getting a poor grade in your class or if there is any other reason you believe he/she should not participate. I appreciate your cooperation. I hope you will see positive results from _____'s participation in this group seminar. Please see me if you have any questions or concerns.

Appendix 1-4

ROTATING SCHEDULE

The schedule for our meetings is listed below.

Day	Date	Topic	Period
Wednesday,	January 29	Goal Setting	1st period
Wednesday,	February 5	Using Resources	2nd period

Wednesday,	February 12	Solving Problems	3rd period
Wednesday,	February 19	Learning Style	4th period
Wednesday,	February 26	Study Schedule	5th period

After A Lunch

Wednesday,	March 5	Communicating	6th period
Wednesday,	March 12	Communicating	1st period
Wednesday,	March 19	Listening	2nd period
Wednesday,	March 26	Summary	3rd period
Wednesday,	May 14	Follow-Up	4th period

Follow-up After A Lunch

Appendix 1-5

SCREENING INTERVIEW

Blum, 1983

1. Define group counseling.
2. Indicate the duration and frequency of the group sessions.
3. Define the member's role within the group.
4. Discuss the kinds of goals group members may desire.
5. Discuss the importance of confidentiality.
6. Obtain a commitment to attend regularly if selected.
7. Determine if the candidate has had other group experience.
8. Determine the intensity of interest and the desire the candidate has for growth.
9. Determine the reason the person desires to be a member.
10. Determine if the candidate can contribute to the group process and the growth of the other group members.
11. Determine the relationships the candidate has with other potential members which may affect the trust within the group (avoid neighborhood effect).

Appendix 1-6

GROUND RULES

1. Attendance. Attend regularly
2. Promptness. Be on time.
3. Honesty. Be honest. Pass from any activity that is embarrassing or particularly difficult for you.
4. Participation. Listen to every member. Share your thoughts. Give helpful feedback when appropriate.

5. Responsibility. Do class assignments ahead of time that are due the day of the group, and submit them to the teacher before missing class for group.
6. Confidentiality. Do not repeat or refer to anything that is said by another group member. You may repeat your goals, how you are working on them, and what *you* say in the group.
7. Work. Actively work to achieve the goals of the group and your individual goals.

Appendix 1-7

GOAL SETTING CRITERIA

Adapted from Napier & Gershenfeld, 1973

1. Is the goal specific enough for you to begin planning and take action?
2. Is the goal specific enough for you to see progress?
3. Is the goal realistic?
4. Can the goal be achieved or at least progress be observed within the time frame of the group?
5. Is the goal something you can change about yourself without depending on change from anyone else?
6. Can other group members help you work to achieve the goal?
7. Is the goal something you really want to achieve?

Appendix 1-8

SESSION EVALUATION

SESSION 1
TODAY I LEARNED _____

SESSION 2
TODAY I LEARNED _____

SESSION 3
TODAY I LEARNED _____

SESSION 4
TODAY I LEARNED _____

SESSION 5
TODAY I LEARNED _____

Improve Academic Performance 17

SESSION 6
TODAY I LEARNED _____

Appendix 1-9

CONNECT THE DOTS ACTIVITY

Rokeach, *The Open and Closed Mind*,
N.Y., Basic Books, 1960.

Display the nine dots on a poster. Ask students to make a similar drawing and then connect the dots without raising the pencil from the paper.

•　　　•　　　•

•　　　•　　　•

•　　　•　　　•

Solution: Illustration 1-1. Insert Here.

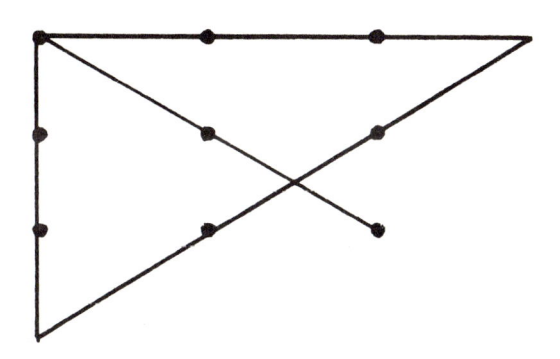

Appendix 1-10

PROBLEM SOLVING MODEL

1. Identify the problem and the person who owns the problem.
2. Clarify the problem until it is fully understood.

3. Generate all alternatives. Brainstorm solutions.
4. Evaluate solutions. Look at the long range and short range consequences of each solution.
5. Eliminate unsatisfactory solutions.
6. Choose one solution.
7. Implement this solution.
8. Make a commitment and set a time to evaluate the results of the solution.

Appendix 1-11

HOW I PROCESS INFORMATION

Beemer, *Study Smarter, Not Harder*
Fairfax, Excel, 1987.
Reprinted by Permission

Directions: Complete the sentences by choosing the response that best describes you. Circle your response.

1. I prefer to learn a new game by:
   a. reading the instructions before starting to play.
   b. listening to somebody explain the instructions.
   c. "jumping right in" and learning as I play.
2. I prefer to learn new material in class by:
   a. reading the textbook myself.
   b. listening to the instructor.
   c. "doing something" with the material, such as a project.
3. As for taking notes, I believe that:
   a. taking notes from the textbook or when the instructor is talking really helps me to learn.
   b. taking notes is really a waste of time because I never use them.
   c. taking notes can be helpful but only if I can put them in a form (pictures, diagrams) that means something to me.
4. As for reading, I believe that:
   a. reading is one of the things I enjoy the most.
   b. reading is one of the things I enjoy least.
   c. reading is enjoyable and worthwhile if the material really interests me.

If you chose response "a" most frequently, you probably like to process information visually. If, on the other hand, you chose "b" more often, you probably process information through hearing. If "c" is the most common response, you probably learn best through feeling it physically.

Appendix 1-12

SATISFYING LEARNING EXPERIENCES

Adapted from Hawley, Simon and Britton,
Composition for Personal Growth.
Amherst, Education Research Associates, 1983.
Reprinted by Permission.

1. Think of the four most satisfying learning experiences you have ever had. These may or may not be part of your school experience. You may write about learning to ride a bike or learning to tie your shoe.
2. On a card, number to four and list each of the four experiences next to a number.
3. After listing all four experiences, think about each experience and, on the worksheet, put the number of the experience, one, two, three or four, next to the statement that applies to that experience.
4. Count the number of experiences that apply to each statement on the worksheet.
5. Review the worksheet and your list of satisfying experiences. On the back of the worksheet, write a few sentences describing your most satisfying learning styles.

Worksheet

	1	2	3	4	Total
I acquired INFORMATION					
I acquired CONCEPTS					
I acquired SKILLS					
I was PHYSICALLY IN MOTION					
I gained power over THINGS					
I gained power over PEOPLE					
I gained power over MYSELF					
I knew in ADVANCE what I wanted to learn					
I PERSEVERED					
I used an OUTSIDE EVALUATION					
I proved myself to MYSELF					
I impressed OTHERS					
I received a TANGIBLE AWARD					

Appendix 1-13

HOPE CHEST

Adapted from Trotzer, *The Counselor and the Group*
Muncie, Accelerated Development, 1989.
Reprinted by permission.

Directions: Ask group members to consider their hopes and wishes for every other member in the group. Distribute sheets of paper and ask them to write at the top, "Hope Chest for (Their Name)." Circulate the papers around the circle.

Each member draws a symbol or writes words to represent his/her specific hopes or wishes for the member whose name is at the top of the paper. Continue the process until each person in the group has made an entry on each paper. When the papers are returned to their originators, members in turn hold up their "Hope Chest" and the other members explain the symbol they drew.

Appendix 1-14

EVALUATION OF THIS SEMINAR

Directions: Using the "Today I Learned" cards and colored pencils or felt pens:
1. Mark with a red "x" and underline in red any statements about learning to talk or communicate.
2. Mark with a blue "x" and underline in blue any statements about learning how to study.
3. Mark with a green "x" and underline in green any statement about keeping track of your grades.
4. Mark with an orange "x" and underline in orange if you wrote that anyone in this group helped you learn how to improve your grades.
5. If you raised your grade(s) this quarter as a result of involvement in this seminar, please write a short note to your parents, teacher, and counselor and inform them about what you did in the group that helped you raise your grades. The leader will make copies for you.

REFERENCES

Beemer, Lynda: *Study Smarter, Not Harder: The Instructor's Guide.* Fairfax, Excel, 1987.

Blum, Dorothy J.: Group leadership training: An inclusive model. *Journal for Specialists in Group Work.* 8(2); 76–85, May 1983.

Hawley, R. C., Simon, S. B. & Britton, D. D.: *Composition for Personal Growth: A*

Teaching Handbook of Meaningful Student Writing Experiences. Amherst, Education Research Associates, 1983.

Napier, Rodney W. & Gershenfeld, Matti K.: *Groups, Theory and Experience.* Boston, Houghton Mifflin, 1973.

Rokeach: *The Open and Closed Mind.* N.Y., Basic Books, 1960.

Trotzer, James: Activity conducted with counselors at Fairfax, Virginia. 1983.

Chapter Two

COUNSEL THE GIFTED

PERFECTIONISM OF GIFTED HIGH SCHOOL STUDENTS

Eleanor Saslaw

Rationale

A characteristic of many gifted students is identified in the literature as "perfectionism." Gifted children often are overly self-critical. They are disappointed if their behavior or performance falls short of their personal goals, and as a result, gifted children often feel inadequate. Authors Webb, Meckstroth and Tolan (1982) state,

> Gifted children easily fall into the trap of being perfectionists even when they are not pressured by others. They set high standards for themselves, even when they do not have the skills to meet these standards, so what objectively is unusual achievement may be interpreted by the child as failure.

Often parents reward performance and achievement to the degree that mental giftedness becomes the child's sole measuring stick. A child may get the idea that if he/she does not produce "A's" or talented performance every time, that he/she is not valued. Hence feelings of worthlessness arise.

Gifted students need to recognize and accept their own abilities, interests and limitations. The gifted student often sets inappropriate goals and then experiences feelings of failure when he/she can't achieve them. Whether the initial pressure is internal or external, the striving to be perfect becomes internalized and thus perfection, an impossible goal, is not achieved. Lack of perfect achievement is seen as failure.

Judy Galbraith (1983) devotes an entire chapter in her book the *Gifted Kid's Survival Guide,* to defining and dealing with perfectionism. She discusses others' expectations, unrealistic self-expectations and how to deal with perfectionism using a practice she calls leveling. She tells the readers "It's absolutely stupid to try to be perfect... First of all, we can't be perfect. Michelangelo was a pretty fair painter, for example, but his math was shabby by comparison...." She puts the problem of perfectionism in proper perspective.

Melissa Klima (1984) has established that group counseling is a positive way to work with the gifted to help them listen to and recognize the contributions of others. This method of working with the gifted has been neglected and not used as often as it could be to help these young people. This group seminar is designed to meet the needs of gifted students.

The goal for this group is to help gifted students develop positive self-concepts, and work through the stress that results from demanding perfectionism of themselves. This seminar is *not* for gifted students who procrastinate, or who use excuses for not doing their best work.

Goal

Members of this seminar will develop positive self-concepts. To achieve this goal, the leader has specific objectives.

Objectives of the Leader

- Define perfectionism.
- Help each student identify the particular form perfectionism takes for him/her.
- Facilitate the sharing of personal feelings related to the stress of perfectionism.
- Foster an understanding that others have similar feelings and experiences related to the pressure of perfectionism.
- Help students clarify, recognize and understand the demands and effects of perfectionism.
- Help students learn to confront and cope with personal feelings and behaviors related to perfectionism.
- Help members develop positive thoughts about themselves, their goals, their errors and themselves.
- Reinforce positive behavior patterns, realistic self-evaluations and realistic goals.

Definition of the Group

This seminar of eight sessions is designed for ten to twelve identified gifted male and female students in grades nine and ten. The group meets weekly for one class period on a rotating basis. Students secure both parental and teacher permission to participate. The final session is scheduled two weeks after the seventh session to assess the changes of attitude and behavior after the group experience.

The seminar is described in the classes for the gifted by previous seminar members who speak about their experience as a participant. Group members are referred by themselves, their teachers, parents, counselors or other school staff.

Seminar participants must be identified as gifted and talented, and must have experienced the stress of perfectionism. They must not be exhibiting stress intense enough to require referral to a clinical psychologist or therapist.

Screening Interview of the Gifted

The leader individually interviews and screens potential group members. Specific information about this seminar is provided, and during the interview the leader makes decisions. In addition to the guidelines in Appendix 1-5, the leader uses the interview to:

1. Clarify and identify the potential member's goal.
2. Determine if and how the group can help in meeting the member's identified goal.
3. Determine if the student is apt to use this group experience as an excuse to not do his/her best work.

Selected members are notified verbally and in writing (Appendix 2-1). Members, teachers and parents are given a schedule (Appendix 1-4). Teachers are requested to acknowledge awareness and permission. Students who are not selected are informed personally and are considered for future group counseling sessions.

Direct personal or telephone contact with parents of selected members is made to explain the purpose, duration and goal for the group. A follow-up permission letter (Appendix 1-2) is sent to further explain the group and request signed permission for the student to participate. The counselor attempts to foster complete understanding of the group's goals and purpose to avoid parental and/or student dissatisfaction which would impede progress once the group is formed.

Plan for the Group Sessions

Session 1

Objectives for Members:
- Become acquainted with each other.
- Begin to trust each other.
- Discuss rules and parameters.
- Review the purpose of the group (group goal).
- Clarify the necessity for confidentiality.

Procedure of the Counselor:
1. Lead the icebreaker, an introduction exercise. Divide group members into dyads. The dyad partners visit with each other for five minutes and during that time each tells the other three facts they consider important in describing themselves. After five minutes members return to the group and they introduce their dyad partner to the entire group by describing their partner the same way they first heard it themselves. The members who are described may add to or clarify what their partners said after the introduction.
2. Introduce the content. Using "Questions and Guidelines" (Appendix 2-2), initiate a discussion of goals, parameters, ground rules and the necessity of confidentiality. Add particular information about this seminar. State that they may gain an understanding of the "problem of perfectionism" and how it relates to them personally, and may learn strategies to help them deal not only with perfectionism, but with other issues as well.

   Members identify a famous person or character from history, television, movies or a book whom they would most like to be like. They tell the group the name of the person and why they would like to be like that person. Other members ask questions or comment.
3. Summarize the session and ask members to complete the form to provide "Group Feedback" (Appendix 2-3).

Session 2

Objectives for Members:

- Briefly review goals, purpose, parameters, rules and confidentiality.
- Continue to get to know each other.
- Define perfectionism and the "problem" of perfectionism.

Materials: A poster with the rules, goals and statement of confidentiality.

Procedure of the Counselor:

1. Lead the icebreaker. Ask members to continue the activity started last session, "Who Do I Wish To Be Like?"
2. Introduce the content. Ask group members to state their personal concept of perfectionism. Begin the process by stating your concept of perfectionism. List ideas on the board, and add to the list as the members verbalize their concepts of perfectionism. Group members may develop a group definition.
3. Administer "How Much of a Perfectionist Are You?" (Appendix 2-4). Suggest that students score their own questionnaires, and rate their place on the perfectionism continuum. Ask students to discuss whether this exercise revealed any insights about themselves or helped them define their personal form of perfectionism.
4. Ask members to read and respond to the differences between the pursuit of excellence and perfectionism as listed by Adderholdt-Elliott (Appendix 2-5). Allow members to relate feelings and incidents that have personal relevance in delineating differences between excellence and perfectionism.
5. Ask for a volunteer to summarize the session. Members then complete anonymously, the group feedback form (Appendix 2-3).

Session 3

Objectives for Members:

- Review definition(s) of perfectionism as discussed in the previous session.
- Identify and define the specific form of perfectionism that causes individual problems.
- Express feelings, frustrations and attitudes caused by the desire for perfectionism.

Materials: Bingo cards (Appendix 2-6). Copies of the poem, *Adam and Me*, (Appendix 2-7), and *The Gifted Kid's Survival Guide* (Galbraith, 1983).

Procedure of the Counselor:

1. Lead the icebreaker "Modified Bingo Game" (Appendix 2-6) to brainstorm ideas about perfectionism. The members approach other members of the group and ask them individually if particular descriptions apply to them. Members sign their names on others' Bingo cards in squares where the descriptions apply. Participants attempt to complete one vertical, horizontal, or diagonal line to be the first to acquire "Bingo." The members then return to the circle to discuss their individual feelings and attitudes as to how perfectionism affects them.
2. Introduce the content. Give students the poem *Adam and Me* (Appendix 2-7). Begin group discussion of the poem by explaining what it means to you, the leader. Ask students to evaluate Adam's perspective and then Adam's parent's perspective. Ask members to relate the poems to a personal experience of theirs. In particular, discuss what Mrs. Carlson means when she says, "For without risk or effort, the loser is you!"
3. Assign homework. Students may take home copies of *The Gifted Kid's Survival Guide* (Galbraith, J. 1983). Tell them to read chapter seven. Ask members to bring their copies of this book with them to the next group session. Ask a volunteer to summarize the session and request that all members complete the form for group feedback at the end of this session.

Session 4

Objectives for Members:

- Summarize the objectives from the previous session.
- Define the personal form of perfectionism that causes individual problems.
- Express feelings about the effects and frustrations with particular situations involving perfectionism.
- Brainstorm and discuss possible ways of confronting and dealing with personal forms of perfectionism.

Materials: Copies of *The Gifted Kid's Survival Guide* (Galbraith 1983).

Procedure of the Counselor:

1. Lead a discussion of chapter seven, "Perfectionism: Is It Possible To Be Perfect?" Review the seven leveling tips for dealing with perfectionism and the various influences (parents, teachers, peers) that we sometimes allow to control our thoughts about ourselves. Help students verbalize a particular area they would like to work on related to perfectionism.
2. Conduct the activity. Use a modified form of Sisk's, (1985) "Child Study Technique."
   a. Distribute a card to each group member. Have each member write down the particular form of perfectionism that he/she would like to address and how it affects him/her.
   b. Explain the rules of brainstorming. Think and record quickly with no negatives or put-downs, regardless of how silly it may seem at the time.
   c. Read your (the counselor's) list first. Ask the rest of the group to brainstorm solutions (sensible or not). Ask a volunteer to read his/her card. Another volunteer writes each solution on the chalkboard as quickly as possible. You remain silent during the time others are providing solutions.
   d. When the brainstorming is completed, and there is a list of possible solutions on the board, systematically evaluate each idea, and ask members to state whether or not it is feasible, if it has been tried, and whether they think it could work for them. As ideas are deleted, they are crossed out.
   e. Ask members to select one idea or solution that they think might work. Suggest that they pledge to try the solution and report back to the group during session seven or before, as to whether or not it was helpful.
3. Ask a volunteer to summarize this session and ask all members to complete the group feedback form (Appendix 2-3).

Sessions 5 and 6

Objective for Members:

- Brainstorm possible solutions to confront and deal with the personal effects of perfectionism.

Procedure of the Counselor:
1. Continue the modified "Child Study Technique" (Sisk, 1985), giving each group member an opportunity to volunteer.
2. Ask a member to summarize the session and ask all members to complete the group feedback form for this session (Appendix 2-3).

Session 7

Objectives for Members:
- Evaluate the selected solutions as to the present and possible future success and effect.
- Explore additional solutions for personal use.
- Apply the solutions over the next two weeks and beyond.

Procedure of the Counselor:
1. Introduce the content by giving each member an opportunity to discuss the results of his/her plan or solution over the past week(s). Encourage members to express, explore and conjecture the effects and the events that may have been altered as a result of their trials. Ask members about their personal feelings and their perceptions of the reactions of others. Other group members may comment, react and suggest.
2. Assign dyads to discuss what each has learned in relation to self and perfectionism. Ask dyad partners to clarify and/or modify personal goals/solutions to be worked on during the next two weeks.
3. Ask a member to summarize the session. Allow students to arrange for refreshments for the final meeting.

Session 8
(Two weeks after Session 7)

Objectives for Members:
- Summarize group and individual achievements.
- Express positive and negative feedback concerning the group, the individual growth and the accomplishment of the group goal, developing a positive self-concept.
- Express future plans and goals and discuss the influence the group

may have had in helping members formulate their goals and change their attitudes and/or behavior.

Procedure of the Counselor:

1. Introduce the content by leading the "Future Projection Exercise" (Corey and Corey, 1988). Ask members to imagine that it is one year and then five years in the future and the group is meeting for a reunion. What would they most hope to be able to say to the group about their lives, the changes they have made and the influence the group had on them? Conduct the activity, "Hope Chest" (Appendix 1-13).
2. Summarize and ask all members to complete the "Final Evaluation" (Appendix 2-8).

Appendix 2-1

NOTICE TO PARTICIPANTS

Date

To: _____
From: _____, Counselor
Re: Group Counseling Seminar

The group counseling seminar will begin on _____ day, _____ ____, period ____. We will meet in Room _____. A schedule of our meetings is attached. Please be prompt to each session. Notify your teachers in ADVANCE when you will miss their class because it is your responsibility to make up work that you miss.

I look forward to meeting with this group. Please let me know if you have any questions.

REMINDER: BE SURE TO TURN IN YOUR PERMISSION FORMS TO ME OR TO THE SECRETARY IN THE GUIDANCE OFFICE.

Appendix 2-2

QUESTIONS AND GUIDELINES

What is group counseling?

Group counseling can mean many things to many people, but it provides an opportunity to:

1. talk about common concerns or problems.

2. express your feelings in a small group with people you can trust.
   3. help you to understand how you are seen by others.

How often do we meet?

This seminar will meet one period a week for seven weeks and then return two weeks later for the last and eighth week. Meetings will begin on time and end on time.

Who is going to be in the group?

There will be ten to twelve freshmen and sophomores who have expressed an interest in participating. One counselor will be the group leader.

Why was I asked to be in this group?

Your counselor can explain the reason(s) you were asked to be in the group. However, if you participate in the group, you may be better able to see and develop your potential.

What can I gain from being in a group?

1. You may better understand others in the group.
2. Understanding others may help you see and evaluate yourself more clearly.
3. You may gain an understanding of the "problem of perfectionism" and how it relates to you personally.
4. You may learn strategies to help you deal with this issue and other issues that may concern you.
5. You may gain an understanding of your strengths and benefit from these.
6. You will have a safe place to express yourself and your true feelings.
7. You will find that others have similar feelings and concerns and that you are not alone in these concerns.

What will be expected of me?

The group will expect of you to:

1. attend regularly and on time.
2. be honest. Pass from any activity that is threatening or causes you anxiety.
3. listen non-judgmentally to other members.
4. be willing to talk about your feelings and things that concern you.
5. show respect by keeping the confidences of other group members and not referring outside the group, to anything they say.
6. be responsible for classwork and assignments and submit these to the teacher before missing class for group meetings.

Appendix 2-3

GROUP FEEDBACK

Session 1, 2, 3, 4, 5, 6, 7

Date _____

1. How do you feel about this session?
   very dissatisfied ____ somewhat dissatisfied ____
   neither satisfied nor dissatisfied ____
   very satisfied ____ somewhat satisfied ____
2. How do you feel about the group so far?
   very dissatisfied ____ somewhat dissatisfied ____
   neither satisfied nor dissatisfied ____
   very satisfied ____ somewhat satisfied ____
3. Please comment on the reason you feel this way.
   _____
   _____

4. Have there been any times when you wished to speak but did not?
   never ____ a few times ____
   fairly often ____ most of the time ____
5. What things HELPED you take part in the session or group? ____
6. What things HINDERED you from taking part in the session or group? ____
   _____

7. How could our next group sessions be improved?
   _____

8. Additional comments _____
   _____

Evaluation of a Session

Circle the words that describe this session:

1. Boring
2. Exciting
3. Revealing
4. Frightening
5. Disturbing
6. O.K.
7. Other _____

Appendix 2-4

HOW MUCH OF A PERFECTIONIST ARE YOU?

Adapted from Adderholdt-Elliott, 1987

Many of you are thinking, "Maybe I am not a perfectionist at all." Would you like to find out? Do you ever feel "I have to please my parents and friends?" "I have to do everything well?" "I want everyone to like me?" This activity will help you find out if you are a perfectionist.

Read each statement, then rate each item according to whether you strongly agree (+2), agree somewhat (+1), can't decide (0), disagree somewhat (−1), or strongly disagree (−2). Answer according to your first thought to get the truest response.

_____ 1. I am critical of people who don't live up to my expectations.
_____ 2. I get upset if I don't finish something I start.
_____ 3. I do things precisely down to the very last detail.
_____ 4. I argue about test scores I don't agree with, even when they won't affect my final grade.
_____ 5. After I finish something, I often feel dissatisfied.
_____ 6. I feel guilty when I don't achieve something I set out to do.
_____ 7. When a teacher hands back one of my papers, I look for mistakes before looking for right answers or positive comments.
_____ 8. I compare my test scores with those of other good students in my class.
_____ 9. It's hard for me to laugh at my own mistakes.
_____ 10. If I don't like the way I've done something, I start over and keep at it until I get it right.

If your total is between +15 and +20, you are too good to be true. Can anybody be this perfect?

If your total is between +10 and +14, you are too good for your own good. You're trying too hard. Why?

If your total is between +5 and +9, you are a borderline perfectionist. In certain conditions you could be a full fledged perfectionist.

If your total is between +1 and +4, you are a healthy pursuer of excellence. You enjoy doing well, but you decide when to pursue excellence.

If your total is between 0 and −5, you are used to hanging loose.

If your total is between −6 and −10, you are a little too relaxed.

If your total is between −11 and −20, you are barely breathing!

Appendix 2-5

EXAMPLES OF THE PURSUIT OF EXCELLENCE VERSUS PERFECTIONISM

"What's the Difference Between Perfectionism and
the Pursuit of Excellence?" excerpt from
Perfectionism: What's Bad About Being Too Good
by Miriam Adderholdt-Elliott, Ph.D. copyright 1987.
Reprinted by permission of Free Spirit Publishing Inc.,
Minneapolis, MN.

The student who pursues excellence does research for a term paper, works hard on it, turns it in on time, and feels good about it.

The perfectionist writes three drafts, stays up two nights in a row, hands the paper in late because he/she had to get it right, and then feels guilty about handing it in late.

The student who pursues excellence studies for a test ahead of time, is confident when taking the test, and feels good about the grade of 96%.

The perfectionist procrastinates for three days, studies the last minute, takes the test with sweaty palms, and feels depressed about the grade of 96% because his/her best friend got a grade of 98%.

The student who pursues excellence chooses to work on group projects because he/she enjoys learning from the varied experiences and approaches of different people.

The perfectionist prefers to work alone because NO ONE can do as good a job as he/she, and the perfectionist is not about to let anyone else slide by on his/her A.

The student who pursues excellence accepts an award with pride even though the engraver misspelled his/her name. He/she knows that it can be fixed at a later date.

The perfectionist accepts the award resentfully because that dumb engraver didn't get his/her name right.

The student who pursues excellence reads the story he/she wrote for the school paper and notices that the editor made some changes to the copy that really improved it.

The perfectionist throws a tantrum because the editor dared to tamper with his/her work.

The student who pursues excellence is willing to try new things, take reasonable risks, and learn from his/her experiences and his/her mistakes.

The perfectionist avoids new experiences because he/she is terrified of making mistakes.

Appendix 2-6

PERFECTION BINGO

(Adapted from Blum, 1982)

TOP ROW ACROSS

1. I worry about getting into a good graduate school.
2. I feel guilty when I take time away from schoolwork to help a friend.
3. I would like to meet more kids like me.
4. I know I cannot be perfect and I still like me.
5. I put pressure on myself to get A's in school.

2ND ROW ACROSS

1. Sometimes I feel like running away.
2. I feel pressure to be good at everything.
3. I still like myself even when I make a mistake.
4. I worry about my future career.
5. I'm O.K. and you're O.K.–even if we are different.

3RD ROW ACROSS

1. I feel pressure from parents to get straight A's.
2. I know I have a right to make mistakes.
3. FREE
4. I cringe if I get a C on a test.
5. I am susceptible to perfection infection.

4TH ROW ACROSS

1. My friends may not like me if I get poor grades.
2. Good friends are important to me.
3. I wish I were better at math.
4. I feel satisfied with myself if I know I have worked hard even if I didn't get an A.
5. I know when I have done a good job.

5TH ROW ACROSS

1. I am afraid I will fail sometimes.
2. I enjoy sports and other activities even if I'm not good.
3. I am involved in extra-curricular activities.
4. I like to socialize a lot.
5. I always enjoy what I do.

Appendix 2-7

ADAM AND ME

Hirschfeld, Adam and Carlson, Jeanne Mobile,
The Gifted Child Today,
1984 Reprinted by permission

It is apparent that I can't do
What it is that you want me to.
So, I agree that your judgement of me
Is not so good so here's the fee.
I promise you that I will pay
the amount needed to get an 'A.'
But if I fail, and get a 'B,'
I hope you won't hang me on the nearest tree.
That is all; this is the end.
Can I count on you to be my friend?
- - - - Adam

A friend, dear Adam, I shall always be;
No frills, no lies, no games from me.
But a teacher, a mentor, purveyor of truth,
These also I must be for you — forsooth
If not, what growth or progress would be?
What future for you to be idle, not free?
To explore all the wonders yet to be found
In our world, the galaxy, questions abound.
And you have the intellect, shame is to waste it!
Knowledge is there, would that you taste it.
Potential is great, but no purpose is gained
If potential lies dormant and intellect's feigned.
Thus your promise I hear, and would hope it rings true,
For without risk or effort, the loser is you!
- - - Adam's Mother

Appendix 2-8

FINAL EVALUATION

Please complete each statement but do not sign this form.

1. Perfectionism is _____, and the form it takes for me personally is _____
_____
_____

2. The group helped me to understand the effects of perfectionism on my self-concept and behavior. (Please indicate whether or not you have discovered or developed new strategies to deal with perfectionism).

_____
_____
_____
_____

3. I do/do not feel that I have discovered some positive steps to deal with the negative stress of perfectionism. Comment:

_____
_____

4. When discussing my concerns and feelings about perfectionism with this group, I felt

_____
_____
_____
_____

5. I would/would not join another seminar because

_____
_____
_____

6. I recommend that the next seminar on perfectionism

_____
_____
_____

7. This seminar has/has not helped me to feel good about myself. (Please comment.)

_____
_____
_____
_____
_____

REFERENCES

Adderholdt-Elliott, Miriam: *Perfectionism: What's Bad About Being Too Good?* Minneapolis, Free Spirit Press, 1987.

Blum, Dorothy J.: *Bingo Game,* Unpublished, 1982.

Carlson, Jeanne and Hirschfeld, Adam: Adam and me. *Gifted Child Today,* 7, (6), 26.

Corey, Gerald and Corey, Marianne: *Groups: Process and Practice.* Monterey, Brooks/Cole, 1988.

Galbraith, Judy: *The Gifted Kid's Survival Guide* (Ages 11–17). Minneapolis, Free Spirit, 1983.

Hirschfeld, Adam and Carlson, Jeanne: Adam and me. *Gifted Child Today,* 7, (6), 26. November/December 1984.

Klima, Melissa: Group counseling, a neglected option for the gifted. *Gifted Children's Quarterly,* Jan/Feb. 1984.

Sisk, Dorothy: *Child Study Technique.* As presented by Largo, Steve, in Counseling the Gifted Course, George Mason University, Spring semester 1985.

Trotzer, James P.: *The Counselor and the Group: Integrating Theory, Training and Practice.* Muncie, Accelerated Development, 1989.

Webb, James, Meckstroth, Elizabeth, Tolan, Stephanie: *Guiding the Gifted Child.* Columbus, Ohio Psychology, 1982.

Chapter Three

DEAL POSITIVELY WITH STRESS

TEST-ANXIETY

Celestine N. Holman

Rationale

Issues facing young people today cause high anxiety. Students must pass competency examinations, standardized tests and college entrance examinations. Many students become so up-tight before major examinations that they miss needed sleep to "cram" in an effort to pass. Some students become ill the day of an examination, and some young people have developed ulcers and other physical problems as a result of anxiety.

Many high school students realize the difficulty, not only of getting accepted by the college of their choice, but also of competing and achieving acceptably in college. Most studies of test-anxiety have been conducted with college students because failures of college examinations often result in students being placed on academic probation or dropped from the college.

Of course it is most important that students master the subject matter, and then acquire the needed skills to perform well on tests. No test-taking techniques can replace daily study and careful review for a test. Attending to the teacher in class, and being alert to the ideas, facts or concepts that the teacher emphasizes, are important skills to prepare adequately for tests.

Some students have inadequate or inaccurate information that causes them anxiety. These students must learn to assert themselves, first to determine the important questions or information they need, and then to find the accurate information. Students may inquire to learn which items will be included in a test. Anxious students may tell themselves that they "can't do that," causing even more anxiety. Sugarman and Freeman (1970) state that anxiety can be an indicator of students' perceived threat to their integrity and personality. If students can affirm their value of self by moving *through* their anxiety instead of fleeing from it, healthy growth can result.

What students say to themselves, their thoughts, and their feelings influence their behavior and the level of their anxiety. These internal statements are referred to as "self-talk."

Relaxation is the antithesis of anxiety; it is psychologically impossible to be relaxed and anxious at the same time. Rose (1977) states that the most commonly used anxiety management procedure is relaxation training. It has been used to treat problems such as insomnia, headaches, back pain, mild forms of depression and generalized anxiety. Therefore it has great value when taught as a skill to students who will be able to adapt and use it throughout their lives.

Katahn, Strenger & Cherry (1966) indicate that students who were involved in their study of test-anxiety, invariably reported that their being able to talk with other students in a group, becoming aware that others had similar problems, and learning better study habits, were the crucial factors in the reduction of anxiety. In this test-anxiety seminar, high school students talk to other students about test-taking, and become aware that others have similar problems. The members learn relaxation techniques, better study habits and good test-taking skills.

Goals

As a result of this group experience members:
- Identify and state the reasons they felt anxiety before or during a test.
- Learn and practice relaxation techniques at appropriate times.
- Demonstrate and use test-taking skills.

Description of the Group

Ten to twelve students from grades ten through twelve, male and female, are selected for this seminar. Teachers and counselors identify students who are particularly anxious when taking a test, who do well on daily work but do not do as well as expected on tests. Two students who have experienced test-anxiety, but now achieve better grades on tests, are the role models for the group. Participation in the seminar is voluntary. The leader describes the goals of the group and explains the reason the student is being considered to participate in this group. The leader further explains and gives examples of activities conducted in this seminar.

The group meets once a week for ten weeks and the sessions are rotated during the school day. The purpose of the group is described to the teachers and a schedule of group sessions is given to the teachers and members. Teachers are invited to comment on any progress of test-taking skills that a member makes after participating in this group. The goals of the seminar are given to parents in a letter.

Session 1

Objectives for the Members:
- Get acquainted with each other.
- Learn the ground rules.

Procedure of the Counselor:
1. Have members introduce themselves and tell about their interests and hobbies. Each member repeats the introduction of the member to their left before introducing themselves.
2. Go over each ground rule of the group and what is expected of each member. A copy of the ground rules (Appendix 1-6) is given to each member.
3. Ask group members if you may have their permission to ask their teachers if they notice a difference in their test-taking skills at the end of the group compared with these skills before they were in the group.
4. Ask members to inform the group as soon as they know they will have a quiz or test in any class. They then can tell the group how they have prepared for the test, and their anxiety level before, during, and after the test.
5. Ask members to relate one of the funniest things that ever happened to them.
6. Summarize the session.

Session 2

Objectives for the Members:
- Learn more about each other and themselves.
- Recognize the anxiety level experienced before, during and after each test.

Procedure of the Counselor:
1. Ask members to recall and summarize what was done in the group last week.
2. Give members the Get Acquainted Bingo Card (Appendix 3-1) and provide directions. A person cannot sign twice until another member signs. After someone else signs, then that member can sign again.
3. Discuss the items on the card and who signed which item.
4. Explain levels of anxiety and the physical manifestations of these levels:
   - (5) Very anxious. Sweaty hands, pounding heart, headache, etc.
   - (4) Somewhat anxious. Breathing hard, afraid they won't remember answers.
   - (3) A little anxious. Worried that they may not know or remember answers.
   - (2) Calm. Assured.
   - (1) Very assured. Anxious to demonstrate what they know about the subject.
5. Ask if any members had a test last week or have a test this week.
6. Ask members to keep a journal of test-taking, and in this journal indicate:
   - The subject in which they have a scheduled test.
   - Each date they have a test.
   - Their level of anxiety
     - (a) before the test,
     - (b) during the test, and
     - (c) after a test.
7. Ask each member to relate something in their life that causes them anxiety. The leader does this first, and then asks for volunteers.
8. Summarize the session.

Session 3

Objective for the Members:

- Become more aware of feelings related to anxiety.

Procedure of the Counselor:

1. Request a volunteer to review the last session.
2. Discuss anxiety provoking situations.
3. Distribute copies of the "Anxiety Scale" (Appendix 3-2)

    Tell students that this is *not* a test and they are not asked to write any answers but just look at it this session. Assure them that they will not be asked to give any answers aloud if they do not want to. Tell them that you will return the scales to them next week, and discuss in general what different answers may show. Collect the blank anxiety scales and save them for the discussion next week.

4. Ask a member to summarize the session.

Session 4

Objective for the Members:

- Become aware of their own level of anxiety on a written scale.

Procedure of the Counselor:

1. Review the last session.
2. Re-distribute the blank anxiety scales.
3. Discuss the items on the scale and lead the group to discuss which items may show low, moderate or high anxiety. Stress that one item does not mean the person has high anxiety in everything. Also assure the members that there is nothing wrong with high anxiety and the purpose of the group is to help them lower their anxiety. Lower anxiety can make life more relaxed and more fun. Members may become more able to accomplish what they want, and acquire a feeling of fulfillment if they can control their anxiety.
4. Collect the blank anxiety scales.
5. Ask each student to review what he/she learned in the session today.

Session 5

Objectives for the Members:
- Identify particular times of extreme tension for themselves.
- Learn to use relaxation exercises (Appendix 3-4).

Procedure of the Counselor:
1. Ask members to label feelings of anxiety so you can list on newsprint the feelings that surface when members are about to take an important test.
2. Discuss which kind of test and which situations cause the most anxiety.
3. Distribute the Pre-Examination Questionnaire (Appendix 3-3). Ask students to imagine that they are going to take the test that makes them most anxious, and complete the scale as though it were a few minutes before they take that important test. They are seated, have pencils in their hands and the tests are being distributed. Now complete the questionnaire.
4. Invite volunteers to share their answers. Discuss the similarities and differences of their feelings.
5. Work through one of the "Body Relaxation Exercises" (Appendix 3-4) with the group before students return to classes. Give copies to members who request them.
6. Summarize the session.

Session 6

Objectives for the Members:
- Continue to discuss particular individual tension and anxiety.
- Continue to practice the progressive physical release from tension.

Procedure of the Counselor:
1. Using the list of feelings of anxiety on newsprint that were generated during Session 5, encourage each member to construct his/her own hierarchy from the condition that causes the least anxiety (1) to the condition that causes the most anxiety (10). Then practice a physical exercise with the items ranked (1) and progress to those that promote the most anxiety (10).
2. Ask members to practice the body relaxation exercises at home,

and then do those exercises, such as deep breathing, before a test. Ask them to report the results to the group.
3. Ask a member to summarize this session.

Session 7

Objectives for the Members:

- Use test-taking skills.
- Use relaxation techniques.

Procedure of the Counselor:

1. Discuss using test time wisely. Distribute "Twelve Test-Taking Tips" (Appendix 3-5), and review each item.
2. Ask members to record in their test journals (1) the date, (2) the test, (3) the test-taking skills they used, (4) the relaxation techniques they used, and (5) the results.
3. Encourage members to use these suggestions when taking teacher-made tests, and to practice each skill. Ask them to report results to the group.
4. Conclude with one relaxation technique.
5. Ask each member to name one thing that he/she will try to remember from this session.

Session 8

Objectives for the Members:

- Become familiar with the test tips and the relaxation techniques so they can be done naturally.
- Reinforce each other by recalling and relating successful use of these techniques.

Procedure of the Counselor:

1. Ask if anyone had a test this week. If so, which techniques did they remember, and which did they follow? Ask members: "What were the results? How anxious were you on a scale of one to ten?"
2. Review the "Twelve Test-Taking Tips" (Appendix 3-5) and finish with one of the relaxation techniques.
3. Summarize this session.

Session 9

Objectives for the Members:

- Review and add any tips for taking tests.
- Practice relaxation techniques.
- Evaluate the seminar by experiencing test-like conditions.

Procedure of the Counselor:

1. Simulate test-taking conditions. Have tables so members can sit at tables when they come to the group. As they enter, assign members to seats at least three feet apart, and tell them that during this session they will have a test on test-taking skills. First, give them the "Pre-Examination Questionnaire" (Appendix 3-3). After these questionnaires have been collected, distribute the "Short Quiz on Test-Taking Skills" (Appendix 3-6).
2. Discuss feelings (1) when they entered the room, (2) when they were given the Pre-Examination Questionnaire, (3) when they were given the quiz, (4) when they completed the quiz.
3. Tell members that you planned the tenth session to take place after the quarter exams, so you are expecting them to use the techniques they have learned in this group when they take their quarter exams. Also, next time will be a chance for members to evaluate the group.
4. Ask one member to summarize the session.

Session 10
(After Quarter Examinations)

Objectives for the Members:

- Evaluate the progress made during the group sessions.

Procedure of the Counselor:

1. Discuss quarter exams and ask if and when the members used the test-taking techniques. Ask if these techniques were any help in relieving their test-anxiety. Ask if the results of their tests show improvement because of their decreased anxiety.
2. Distribute the evaluation forms (Appendix 3-7) and ask members to complete these forms anonymously.

3. Ask members to identify the most and the least helpful topics in these seminar sessions.
4. Reinforce their learning by telling how each member contributed to the group.
5. Summarize what you believe each member has contributed to the group.

Appendix 3-1

GET ACQUAINTED BINGO CARD

(Adapted from Blum, 1982)

TOP ROW ACROSS:

    Has a dog for a pet
    Lives in an apartment
    Was born in December
    Has lived in another country
    Likes to swim

SECOND ROW ACROSS:

    Wears eye glasses or contacts
    Was born in a state other than VA
    Plans to attend college
    Walks to school
    Was born in another country

THIRD ROW ACROSS:

    Was born in VA
    Works after school
    FREE
    Has dark eyes
    Likes to ski

FOURTH ROW ACROSS:

    Has blonde hair
    Has a younger sister
    Is wearing ear rings
    Drives a car
    Likes to dance

FIFTH ROW ACROSS:

    Plays sports
    Plays a musical instrument
    Has a cat for a pet
    Has an older brother
    Has a younger brother

Appendix 3-2

ANXIETY SCALE ✓

Directions: Answer True (T) or False (F) to items as they apply to you.

_____ I am often sick to my stomach.
_____ I am about as nervous as other people.
_____ I work under a great deal of strain.
_____ I blush as often as others.
_____ I worry quite a bit over possible troubles.
_____ When embarrassed I often break out in a sweat which is annoying.
_____ I do not often notice my heart pounding and I am seldom short of breath.
_____ At times I lose sleep over worry.
_____ My sleep is restless and disturbed.
_____ I often dream about things I don't like to tell other people.
_____ My feelings are hurt easier than most people.
_____ I often find myself worrying about something.
_____ I wish I could be as happy as others.
_____ I feel anxious about something or someone almost all the time.
_____ At times I am so restless that I cannot sit in a chair for long.
_____ I have often felt that I faced so many difficulties I could not overcome them.
_____ At times I have been worried beyond reason about something that really did not matter.
_____ I do not have as many fears as my friends.
_____ I am more self-conscious than most people.
_____ I am the kind of person who takes things hard.
_____ I am a nervous person.
_____ Life is often a strain for me.
_____ I am not at all confident of myself.
_____ I don't like to face a difficulty or make an important decision.
_____ I am confident of myself.

Appendix 3-3

PRE-EXAMINATION QUESTIONNAIRE

DOROTHY J. BLUM

Directions: To the left of each of the following statements indicate your feelings, attitudes, or thoughts as they are right now, using the following numerical scale.

1 — Does not describe my present condition.
2 — Is barely noticeable.
3 — Is moderate.
4 — Is strong.
5 — Is very strong and describes my present condition well.

_____ I feel my heart beating fast.
_____ I feel regretful.
_____ I am so tense that my stomach is upset.
_____ I have a headache.
_____ My stomach aches.
_____ I am afraid that I should have studied more for this test.
_____ I feel uneasy or upset.
_____ I feel that others will be disappointed in me.
_____ I am nervous.
_____ I feel I may not do as well on this test as I could.
_____ I feel panicky.
_____ I do not feel confident about my performance on this test.

Appendix 3-4

BODY RELAXATION EXERCISES

Ask students to sit comfortably in their chairs. Tell them to relax physically by following what you suggest. Tell them that they may have a copy of these exercises to practice at home, before giving a speech, or before taking a test.

Read slowly and evenly. Stop when appropriate until everyone experiences relaxation in that part of their body.

1. Lift your shoulders as close to your ears as possible. Hold the position for ten seconds and then drop your shoulders as low as you can for ten seconds as you take a deep breath. Do this five or six times. Then relax your arms, hands and face. Allow your jaw to drop.
2. Close your eyes, now relax your eyes. Think to relax your eyebrows, now your forehead. Let your jaw drop to open your mouth. Your head may nod forward. Now release all tension from your neck, your shoulders, your left arm followed by your right arm. Feel the tension go from your hand and from your fingers. Relax the stomach muscles. Now release tension from your right leg and toes, now your left leg and toes. Repeat the word "relax" over and over. Feel every inch of your body releasing tension.
3. Imagine you are lying on a huge, soft pillow, resting on a cloud which is drifting in space. You are weightless and your body feels light and free and completely relaxed.
4. Take long, slow, deep breaths. Inhale, hold and then exhale slowly. (This is an excellent technique for getting rid of butterflies in the stomach prior to delivering an important speech, taking a test, or working on a difficult problem).
5. When you are at home and want to relax try taking a long brisk walk. It will tire and at the same time relax you. Soak in a hot tub and repeat exercise two.

Appendix 3-5

TWELVE TEST-TAKING TIPS

Dorothy J. Blum

1. Prepare in Advance. Of course the best preparation for a test is done before the test. Complete assignments on time, read the textbook on schedule or ahead of the lesson to be discussed. Write questions as you read the text and then find the answers by reading, by asking these questions in class, or by asking the teacher after class. Outline assignments that are difficult. Ask questions about content. Other students may have the same questions. Take good notes when the teacher is explaining a problem or is presenting material that the teacher thinks students should learn. Be astute to what the teacher thinks is important and star or highlight this information in your notes. Before the test, review your notes and your textbook. Ask the teacher what the test will cover. Then go through your notes and pick out the things the teacher stressed. Highlight these and be sure to know the answers as you review carefully and purposefully for the test.
2. Listen. Listen carefully to all directions and everything the test administrator says before you start answering questions. Keep directions in mind as you complete the test.
3. Ask questions. If not in the directions, ask how long you have to complete the test and if the right answers are counted or if the wrong answers are subtracted from right answers. This indicates whether you should guess.
4. Do the examples. Work all examples and take these practice items seriously.
5. Scan the test. Look over the entire test before you start to answer any questions. Work all easy items first. Leave blank any items that stump you or that you have to spend a lot of time in computing the answer. You will return to the items you leave blank.
6. Read carefully. Read each item carefully, answer the precise question that is asked. Pay particular attention to key terms in the question.
7. Work accurately and rapidly. Work as rapidly as possible with reasonable assurance of accuracy. Work carefully on those items which yield the most points in a given amount of time.
8. Guess when appropriate. When you have answered all the easy items go back to the beginning and answer those items you left blank. If you can delete all but two answers of a multiple choice item, guess between these two answers.
9. Answer all questions. Attempt to answer every question.
10. Analyze the tough questions. Think through any question that really bothers you, breaking it into sequential steps.
11. Know the question. If a question gives you trouble, translate the material in the question to a different form. Ask what the question really is.
12. Check all answers. Re-read all the questions and check your answers.

Appendix 3-6

SHORT QUIZ ON TEST-TAKING TIPS

Dorothy J. Blum

1. Which items should I complete first? _____

2. Why should I work the examples when they are so easy? _____

3. How should I determine whether I should guess at any items?
   _____
   _____
   _____

4. Why should I first skip the items that take the most time? _____
   _____
   _____

5. Why should I re-read the questions and my answers?
   _____
   _____

Appendix 3-7

EVALUATION OF GROUP TO DECREASE TEST-ANXIETY

1. The reasons I experienced test-anxiety before I participated in this group were _____
   _____
   _____
   _____

2. Test-taking skills that I can use now are _____
   _____
   _____
   _____

3. The relaxation techniques that I can use now are
   _____
   _____
   _____

4. This group helped me to _____
   _____
   _____

5. I do/do not achieve better scores on tests now because _____
_____
_____
_____

REFERENCES

Blum, Dorothy J.: *Bingo.* Unpublished, 1982.
Blum, Dorothy J.: *Pre-Examination Questionnaire.* Unpublished, 1987.
Blum, Dorothy J.: *Twelve Test-Taking Tips.* Unpublished, 1987.
Blum, Dorothy J.: *Short Quiz on Test-Taking Skills.* Unpublished, 1987.
Katahn, M., Strenger, S. & Cherry, N. Group counseling and behavior therapy with test-anxious college students. *Journal of Consulting Psychology, 30:*544–549, 1966.
Rose, S.: *Group Therapy: A Behavioral Approach.* Englewood Cliffs, Prentice-Hall. 1977.
Sugarman, D. & Freeman, L.: *The Search for Serenity: Understanding and Overcoming Anxiety.* London, Collier & MacMillan, 1970.

Chapter Four

HELP NEWCOMERS

NEWCOMERS' SEMINAR

Anita Francis

Rationale

The Newcomers' Seminar is for students who have been up-rooted from previous friends, and are attending a school where they are unfamiliar with their peers, teachers, and the expectations and norms of the school. Young people sometimes resent being uprooted to move to a different town, city, state or country because of circumstances over which they had no control. Any time people are separated from someone or something that is important in their lives, they go through grief, a well-defined set of stages and steps (Lane and Dickey, 1988).

New students often lack the communication skills necessary to talk out their pain of leaving friends and their previous school, where they felt accepted and comfortable (Lane and Dickey, 1988). Many students feel anxious about starting over in a new school. It is particularly hard for adolescents to adjust, to fit in and adapt to new classes and teachers, as well as try to make new friends. Goldberg (1980) noted that adolescents who move are faced with a double stress: the adaptation to a new environment and the pressures of adolescent development. Strother and Harvill (1986) state that adolescents seem to experience the most difficulty with the loss of valued peer relationships because, to adolescents, their friends comprise their most important support system.

Counselors need to understand and address the needs of new students who frequently need special attention and help in getting acquainted. Holland et al (1974) stated that young people who have moved to a new community have been identified as a high-risk group. These authors found that three basic tasks must be resolved for the student to adapt successfully to the new school: (1) the student must find an acceptable place among his/her new peers, (2) the student must be able to meet the academic and behavioral standards for his/her grade level in the new school, and (3) the student must be accepted by the teachers as an appropriate member of his/her classes.

New students indicate that one of the hardest things to do, is to go to the cafeteria for lunch because they feel self-conscious eating alone, yet they don't know anyone. During lunchtime some new students retreat to the library, an empty classroom, or eat with a teacher rather than face the cafeteria full of young people and still feel lonely.

Lane and Dickey (1988) state that the key point for new students is to help them to get involved and help make their adjustment to the new school as smooth as possible. Strother and Harvill (1986) stress that a well-planned group experience can help these new students go through the necessary grieving process, and be ready to make new friends, and adjust to the new school.

Goals

Members will, as a result of this group experience:
- Have someone to eat lunch with.
- Get acquainted with other new students and with student leaders in the school.
- Become acquainted with the academic program and the norms of the new high school; not only the explicit rules, but also the implicit expectations the teachers have of students and the students have of the teachers.
- Learn about the social and club opportunities and how to get involved in these.
- Know specific facts about their new high school.

Definition of the Group

This group may change weekly. Membership is voluntary and open to all students who are new, including students from the English As A Second Language (ESL) program. The registrar or counselor discusses the group with the student and parent(s) when the student registers, and explains that the seminar is a good place to get acquainted and make new friends. The counselor answers questions and a parent permission letter (Appendix 1-2) is given to them. Members of the Newcomers' Seminar are encouraged to participate in six sessions, one class period each week.

The seminar is held on a rotating schedule. The counselor gives the members hall-passes the day before the seminar meets, to remind both the student and the teacher of the group session. After each session, the counselor provides a list of all members who attended the seminar to the teachers. If the member has a test or the teacher believes the student needs to stay in class, then the student must miss the group that week.

Procedures

The ground rules (Appendix 1-6) are explained and a copy is given to each member the first day he/she attends the seminar. The host/hostess, a member who attended the previous session, introduces the new member(s) and explains and shows them what is expected in the seminar. The members give their names, grade levels, the town they moved from, their bus number, and lunch schedule.

After the introductions, the counselor gives directions for an icebreaker, which re-acquaints the returning members, and helps the new members feel a part of the group. Following the icebreaker, the counselor introduces one academic discipline and the members discuss how they are doing in that subject, the teachers' expectations, and how these are similar to or different from the expectations at their previous school. Peer counselors, peer tutors and members of the National Honor Society (NHS) are invited to particular sessions to discuss how to prepare for classes and tests, and to explain teachers' expectations from the students' point of view.

Sessions

Session 1

Guest Speakers: The English department chairperson, the clinic nurse, the librarian, the peer counselors and peer tutors.

Objectives for the Members:
- Become acquainted with each other and the ground rules for the group (Appendix 1-6).
- Learn about the English department requirements, the library, and the clinic.

- Meet the peer counselors (if they haven't met before), and the peer tutors.

Procedure of the Counselor:
1. Lead the name game (Appendix 4-1). After going around with names, students give their grade levels and then something they like to do.
2. Inform students of the ground rules, post them on the wall, and give each student a copy (Appendix 1-6).
3. Introduce the English department chairperson who discusses requirements in English courses. Invite students to discuss any difficulty they are having in an English course.
4. Introduce the peer counselors and peer tutors, who explain their programs, and the procedures to request tutoring help.
5. Give students a map of the school.
6. Conduct a tour of the building so the students know where all classes, the clinic, the library, the lockers, and the restrooms are located. The librarian and clinic nurse explain their procedures.

Summary:
7. After the tour the members reassemble, and tell the group one thing they learned during this session.
8. Remind members of the time they will meet next week.
9. Ask for a volunteer host/hostess for the next session.

Session 2

Guest Speakers: The social studies department chairperson, and a student who discusses school clubs, and the extracurricular program.

Objectives for the Members:
- Have someone with whom to eat lunch each day.
- Learn about the expectations in the social studies department.
- Know about bus schedules, late bus schedules and the extracurricular program in the school.
- Learn about the school clubs and the extracurricular program.

Procedure of the Counselor:

1. Start the name game with number four, (Appendix 4-1). Members give their impression of the new school.
2. Ask members to repeat the name game, giving which lunch period they have, and with whom they eat lunch.
3. If a member does not have a lunch partner, make arrangements for a student who has the same lunch period to join that new student for lunch for three days. Arrange for another student to have lunch with the new student the next three days.
4. Introduce the social studies department chairperson who discusses the expectations of the social studies teachers.
5. Lead a discussion of the bus schedules, bus rules and the late bus schedules.
6. Introduce a student who is involved in a school club who discusses all school clubs and explains the procedures for joining these clubs. Officers of clubs may meet perspective members.

Summary

7. Ask all new students to tell the group which club they would enjoy most, review the procedures to join that club, and indicate whether they want to attend a meeting of that club.
8. Arrange for a host/hostess for next session.

Session 3

Guest Speakers: The mathematics department chairperson and a student who discusses the sports program.

Objectives for the Members:

- Know about the mathematics department and the expectations of the mathematics teachers.
- Know about the sports program: varsity, junior varsity, freshman, and intramural sports.

Procedure of the Counselor:

1. Conduct the name game, indicating again the club in which they are most interested, and if they plan to join how they would begin.
2. Ask if anyone is eating lunch alone. If so, make new arrangements.

3. Introduce the mathematics department chairperson who discusses the expectations in the mathematics courses.
4. Introduce a student who is active in sports, and recommended by the athletic director or coach, who explains the sports program. This student has a list of all sports, competitive and intramural, and a practice schedule with coaches' names and how to get started in each sport.

Summary:
5. Ask all students to name the sport that sounds like the most fun to them and indicate whether or not they want to get involved in that sport this term.

Session 4

Guest Speakers: The science department chairperson, a reporter from the school newspaper, and administrators.

Objectives for the Members:
- Know who the administrators are and what they do.
- Know the expectations of the science teachers.
- Be interviewed for the school newspaper.

Procedure of the Counselor:
1. Lead the name game, numbers three and six (Appendix 4-1).
2. Introduce the reporters from the school newspaper who are invited to this session to write an article about the Newcomers' Seminar and the new students.
3. Introduce the science department chairperson who discusses the science program in the school.
4. Take the new students to the offices of the administrators. Introduce them to each administrator who explains what he/she does in the school.

Summary:
5. Ask members to indicate if they are interested in the sports program. Also ask them to tell the group what they have done to make friends and how successful they have been.

Session 5

Guest Speakers: The foreign language department chairperson, officers of the Student Council Association (SCA), and class officers.

Objectives for the Members:
- Know about the student government of this school.
- Know the officers of the Student Council Association (SCA), and the Freshman, Sophomore, Junior and Senior class officers.
- Have someone with whom he/she feels comfortable to eat lunch.
- Know about the expectations of the foreign language teachers.

Procedure of the Counselor:
1. Lead the name game, numbers five and seven.
2. Introduce the chairperson of the foreign language department who explains the foreign language program.
3. Ask each member to tell about the most difficult thing to do at this school. Members help each other by making suggestions.
4. Ask the invited officers of the Student Council Association (SCA), and class officers to introduce themselves and explain the election procedures and how new students can get involved in SCA and class activities.

Summary:
5. New students review the names of the SCA and class officers, and what was said about particular class activities for their grade level.

Session 6

Guest Speaker: The chairperson of the physical education department.

Objectives for the Members:
- Learn about the physical education department and the expectations of the physical education teachers.
- Evaluate the group sessions.

Procedure of the Counselor:
1. Introduce the chairperson of the physical education department who discusses the requirements of the physical education department.

2. Distribute the evaluation form (Appendix 4-2), and ask members to complete the form.
3. Reinforce how members have progressed through the seminar. Continue to meet with students who wish.
4. The counselor may use other topics listed in Appendix 4-3 if students desire to continue meeting.

Summary:
5. Ask all members to tell one positive thing about every other member in the circle.

Appendix 4-1

NAME GAME AND ADAPTATIONS

Sessions 1-5

Directions: The leader begins by giving his/her name and the name of the person on his/her right. The person to the left of the leader repeats the names of the two people sitting to his/her right, and adds his/her name. Each person in the circle then gives his/her name in turn, repeating the name of each person seated to the right of him/her.

1. My name is _____ and seated to the right of me are _____, _____, and _____.
2. My name is _____ and last period I was in _____ class.
3. At my other school I particularly liked _____.
4. My first impression of this school is/was _____.
5. Something unique about me is _____.
6. The hardest thing for me to do here is _____.
7. The thing I like most about this school is _____.

Appendix 4-2

EVALUATION FORM

Directions: Indicate your answer by circling SA = Strongly Agree, A = Agree, D = Disagree, SD = Strongly Disagree, or writing your answer.

1. I met all students in the group, and I know them by their first names.
   SA A D SD
2. I have had someone with whom to eat lunch every day since I was in the group.
   SA A D SD

3. I now have my own friends, and eat with friends who have the same lunch period as me. SA A D SD
4. I know about the buses, the clinic, the library, the lockers, the schedules, etc. SA A D SD
5. I know what is expected of students in courses in English. SA A D SD
6. I know what is expected of students in courses in social studies. SA A D SD
7. I know what is expected of students in courses in mathematics. SA A D SD
8. I know what is expected of students in courses in science. SA A D SD
9. I know what is expected of students in courses in foreign language. SA A D SD
10. I know what is expected of students in courses in physical education. SA A D SD
11. Something I would like to know more about is _____
12. As a new student, it would have helped me if _____
13. I attended six, five, four, three two, or one sessions _____
14. The most worthwhile discussion for me was _____
15. I would suggest that in future seminars _____

16. This seminar was helpful to me. SA A D SD

Appendix 4-3

POSSIBLE TOPICS FOR NEW STUDENT SEMINARS

FACTS ABOUT THE SCHOOL
1. Manners on the bus
2. How to handle homework
3. How to make up work (tutors, homebound teachers)
4. What to do when you are sick
5. What to do if you get into trouble

SKILLS
1. How to maintain friendships by long distance
2. How to introduce yourself and others
3. How to ask a teacher for help
4. How to stop someone from picking on you

5. How to cope with a teacher who doesn't like you
6. How to make new friends
7. How to deal with problems with friends
8. How to stop comparing the past with the present

REFERENCES

Goldberg, E. R.: Relocation and the family: A crisis in adolescent development. In G. V. Coelho & P. I. Ahmed (Eds.), *Uprooting and Development: Dilemmas of Coping with Modernization.* New York, Plenum. 1980.

Holland, J. V., Kaplan, D. M., and Davis, S. D.: Interschool transfers: A mental health challenge. *Journal of School Health. 44,* 74–79 as cited in Holland-Jacobsen, Susan, Holland, Rosemary P, and Cook, Alicia Skinner: Mobility: Easing the transition for students. *The School Counselor. 32* (1) 49–53, September 1984.

Lane, Kenneth E. and Dickey, Ted: New students and grief. *The School Counselor. 35,* 359–362, May 1988.

Strother, JoAnna and Harvill, Riley: Support groups for relocated adolescent students: A model for school counselors. *Journal for Specialists in Group Work. 11* (2) 114–120, May 1986.

Chapter Five

HELP TEENAGERS OF CHANGING FAMILIES

SEMINAR FOR ADOLESCENTS LIVING WITH PARENTS WHO ARE SEPARATED OR DIVORCED

Marcella C. Aldridge

Introduction

Educators find that a growing proportion of their students come from divorced families. Dr. Paul Glick of the Bureau of Census, predicts that by 1990, 50 percent of all students eighteen years or younger will have lived for some part of their lives in a single-parent home (Peters, 1985).

Divorce brings about the severance of important relationships. Separation of parents can contribute to behavioral, emotional and learning concerns (Elkind, 1984). In a study conducted by Reynolds (Peters, 1985), a correlation was discovered between teens from single-parent homes and records of low grades, truancy, and acting-out behavior. The divorce process or chain of events set in motion by the separation of their parents often makes young people anxious.

Although the support of others can not decrease or take away the pain associated with the parting, the network or group can make the pain more bearable so the parting will not be debilitating to these young people.

School counselors are part of the students' daily environment and can be the most appropriate adults to provide assistance to teen-agers whose families are no longer intact. Sheridan, Baker and de Lissovoy (1984) studied three counseling methods for helping normal adolescents who were experiencing a changing family. Of the three methods: (1) standard individual counseling, (2) structured group counseling, and (3) explicit bibliotherapy, the group counseling and bibliotherapy were noted by the students as being most helpful. This seminar brings students with common needs, feelings, and life experiences together where peer-group interactions can be positive and helpful, and bonding and healing can take place.

This is a structured group experience that includes the bibliotherapy recommended by Sheridan, Baker, and de Lissovoy (1984). Members read the book, *How to Get It Together When Your Parents Are Coming Apart* (Richards and Willis, 1975), and see the filmstrips from *Coping With Family Changes*.

Jane Hammatt-Kavaloski (1982) has written a philosophical framework for a divorce group. These points are stressed:

- The positive aspects of family life should be emphasized. Even though families are not together, many people are making carefully considered choices of life-style. Although change can create stress for the adults and children involved, it can also bring opportunities for growth and insight.
- Schools should eliminate the stigma and negative stereotypes that often accompany terms such as "broken-home" or "single-parent family." Single-parent families only exist when one parent has died or when one parent has no contact whatsoever with the child.
- Significant changes other than divorce affect the lives of children and should not be overlooked.
- A preventive program (group counseling program) for all children, whether or not they are experiencing a family change, should be developed.

Goals

The following goals have been suggested for "Divorce Groups" by Green (1978):

1. Facilitate interaction and support among students who are experiencing separation or divorce of parents.
2. Inform the teen-agers of the realistic facts regarding divorce.
3. Help members clarify, recognize, and understand feelings and emotions of themselves and their parents pertaining to the divorce.
4. Help members learn how to confront and cope with problems specific to the divorce.
5. Help members deal with personal relationships of friends and family.

6. Help members develop positive self-images and broaden their range of interests.
7. Help members develop rational, correct thoughts regarding themselves and divorce.
8. Help members change existing negative behavior patterns to more positive ways of acting.

Setting goals enhances commitment and involvement of all members toward open sharing and growth. The goals for this seminar are:

- Facilitate communication among members.
- Provide emotional support to members.
- Help members to learn from others' experiences how to cope with problems arising from the separation/divorce of natural parents.

Definition of the Group

The purpose of this seminar is to provide a supportive, non-judgmental atmosphere in which students can express their feelings. Eight sessions are designed for ten to twelve students in grades ten to twelve who have parents who are separated, divorced, or remarried. The group includes males and females of different cultural backgrounds.

Selection of Group Members

Prospective members are referred by teachers, counselors, parents or students. Referrals also come from graduates of this seminar who identify their friends who are experiencing changes in their families. This seminar is not structured to meet the needs of students who exhibit severe emotional disturbance. Potential members of the seminar are screened individually (Appendix 1-5).

Parental Advocacy

The counselor informs all selected members and gives them a letter inviting their parents to a meeting to explain the purpose of the seminar (Adapted from Appendix 1-2). During this meeting parents meet each other, review the materials, and discuss concerns with the counselor before the students meet. If a parent meeting is not feasible, the counselor calls the parents to explain the purpose of the seminar and to relieve any anxiety the parents may have about their sons/daughters being members of this seminar. Parents can give their permission if they cannot attend the meeting. Parents become cooperative and strong advocates of the seminar when they are informed, and when they realize that the purpose of the seminar is to help the students adjust to their changing life-styles, and increase the members' understanding of the feelings of their parents during this painful process.

Sessions

Session 1, Introduction to the Seminar

Objectives of the Leader
- Help members become acquainted with each other.
- Begin a foundation for comfort, trust, and group cohesiveness.
- Set rules and parameters for the seminar.
- Review seminar goals.

Procedure of the Leader
1. Conduct the icebreaker, "Get Acquainted Bingo" (Appendix 3-1).
2. Lead a discussion about the completion of the card to introduce members to each other.
3. Explain the purpose of the seminar. Stress that although there is a plan for each session, it is more important that members discuss what is happening in the present. Each session begins with an opportunity to share current feelings.
4. Talk about the ground rules, (Appendix 1-6). Distribute copies to each member.
5. Give a short introduction to goal setting. Talk about the seminar goals, then discuss individual objectives. What would the members like to achieve from being in this seminar?
6. Discuss one personal objective that you, the counselor, will work on during the duration of the seminar. This may be to improve your relationship with one person.
7. Ask each person to think about a personal objective during the next two weeks.
8. Explain the topic for next week.

Session 2, You and Your Family

Objectives of the Leader

- Re-emphasize the ground rules for the seminar.
- Help group members continue to become better acquainted with each other.
- Develop a "picture" of each member's family and social environment.

Procedure of the Leader

1. Distribute cards and a pencil. Ask members to list the names of as many seminar members as they can and one detail that they remember about each person.
2. Review names and discuss remembering names.
3. Conduct the activity. Remind members that they may pass from any activity if they feel embarrassed or uncomfortable doing it. The activity, "Dinner Table" helps members think about their own families and begin to think about the similarities with other families as well.
   a. Distribute a sheet of paper to each member and give directions. "Draw a circle representing your dinner table. At this table represent each female by a circle, each male by a triangle and put the figures where these family members usually sit at the table. Draw a figure for yourself where you sit at this table and include others who are at or near the table such as personal friends, family friends, etc. You may draw more than one table if you have more than one family."
   b. Ask each member to describe the table(s) he/she has drawn and explain the relationships within his/her family.
   c. If members do not relate to a dinner table, they may draw their family tree. On the branches of the tree they put a circle or a triangle with the name of each member of the family that they have known, not just heard about.
4. Give each member a copy of *How to Get It Together When Your Parents Are Coming Apart* (Richards & Willis, 1976) to be returned at the eighth session.

Session 3, Setting Individual Objectives

Objectives of the Leader
- Help members agree on the goals for the seminar.
- Enable members to express their personal feelings about divorce.

Procedure of the Leader
1. Summarize the first two sessions.
2. Give copies of the list of eight goals to members (Green, 1978), and ask them to rank order these goals in the order of importance to them, with eight being of great importance and one being of little importance. Tally the rank orders of these goals and plan sessions to address the three goals given highest priority by the members.
3. Distribute questionnaires (Appendix 5-1) to members. State that any member may refrain from answering any question. Items are discussed only when members feel comfortable discussing them.
4. Discuss items that members want to discuss.
5. Provide directions for the activity, "Family Sculpture."
    a. Each member in turn selects other members of the group to represent significant others in his/her life. The focus member then places the selected members around the room to represent distance or closeness to him/her, first the way it is, and then the way he/she would like it to be.
    b. The focus member then describes his/her family and his/her feelings about this distance.
    c. Members may pass if they wish.
6. Tell the members that next week members can talk about some of the feelings mentioned in this session.

Session 4, Expressing Feelings

Objectives of the Leader
- Encourage students to express their perceptions and feelings.
- Encourage students to identify their feelings and possible reasons for their feelings.
- Enable members to share their feelings with others.

Procedure of the Leader:

1. Conduct the activity, "Projective Drawing." Show a picture of a teen-ager. Give each member a card and pencils. Ask members to respond to the following questions:
   a. What is the teen-ager thinking?
   b. What is the teen-ager feeling?
   c. What is the teen-ager saying?
2. Ask seminar members to discuss their answers in groups of four or five members. Then the entire group discusses the following questions:
   a. Why is it important to know how someone else is feeling?
   b. Has someone ever misunderstood how you felt? Were you able to tell them your feelings?
   c. Are there ways that you can better understand how someone else is feeling?
3. Distribute the list of feeling words (Appendix 5-2). Ask members to think of a recent event in their lives. It may be happy or sad, and then circle the words that describe their feelings when they are happy or sad.
4. Suggest that students list the feeling words as they read the book (Richards & Willis, 1976).
5. Request that they bring these copies of "Feeling Vocabularies" to the next two sessions when the group views filmstrips.

Sessions 5 and 6, Talking About Divorce

Objectives of the Leader

- Enable members to increase their understanding of the impact the divorce has had upon their parents as well as upon themselves.
- Assist seminar members to recognize the differences and similarities of divorce situations.
- Provide support for seminar members.

Procedure of the Leader

1. Show one filmstrip from the set *Coping With Family Changes* (Sunburst, 1983), and discuss it before showing the next filmstrip. Start with Part I, "Redefining the Family." These filmstrips and

cassettes are a stimulus for discussion during this session and the next.
2. Lead a discussion focusing on the similarities and differences of the characters depicted in the films. Then focus the discussion on the similarities and differences of members within the group. After discussing the first filmstrip show Part II, "Single-Parent Families" and discuss this before showing Part III, "Step-parents and Blended Families."
3. Ask members to finish reading the book, *How to Get It Together When Your Parents Are Coming Apart* (1976) before the next session so it can be discussed in terms of what can be learned from the author.
4. Tell the members that next week they may present personal problems anonymously to get assistance from other members.

Session 7, Working Through and Coping with Problems

Objectives of the Leader

- Help seminar members discriminate between solvable and unsolvable problems.
- Help seminar members share their concerns about the divorce of their parents.
- Provide suggestions for problem solving.

Procedure of the Leader

1. Ask members to select one part of the book that was similar to or different from their situation, and discuss how it is similar or different. Then ask for their evaluation of the book.
2. Give cards and pencils to members and invite them to write any problem on the card that has not been discussed in the group. Tell them not to put their names on the cards and that these problems will be discussed anonymously.
3. Collect all cards and ask members to brainstorm suggestions for each concern that you read aloud from the card.
4. Suggest that a problem be role-played.
5. After a role-play, a member may identify his/her concern, and request more specific help. The member then may rehearse the

behavior he/she wants to apply to the situation. This assists the member to carry out the solution in real life.
6. Remind members that next week will be the last weekly session and ask them to return the book, *How to Get It Together When Your Parents Are Coming Apart.*

Session 8, Review and Termination of the Seminar

Objectives of the Leader

- Summarize the achievements made during the seminar.
- Evaluate the growth of seminar members.
- Consolidate learning as applied to problems of divorce.
- Ask members to express positive and negative feedback about the group experience as it was for them.

Procedure of the Leader

1. Distribute pencils and the "Evaluation" (Appendix 5-3).
2. Ask members to evaluate their experience in this seminar.
3. Conduct the activity "Hope Chest" (Appendix 1-13).
4. Remind members of the date for the last meeting.

Session 9, Get-Together with Refreshments (One Month After Session 8)

Procedure of the Leader:

1. Ask each member to relate his/her progress, what he/she has accomplished since the last meeting.
2. Ask each member to complete the "Seminar Evaluation" (Appendix 5-4).
3. Distribute the respective previous evaluations (Appendix 5-3) to members. Ask them if they see differences in their answers after one month. Discuss.
4. Ask members for their permission to share with the guidance director and/or principal, their evaluations of the seminar. These results can point out the value of the group experience as expressed by members, so the seminar can be offered again to other students.

Appendix 5-1

QUESTIONNAIRE

(Adapted from Allers, 1982)

1. How long have your parents been divorced? _____
2. Have you discussed the divorce with your Mom? _____ Y _____ N
   with your Dad? _____ Y _____ N
3. Did your parents tell you why they became divorced? _____ Y _____ N
4. Do you feel you understand why your parents became divorced?
   _____ Y _____ N
5. Do you believe it was a good idea for your parents to divorce?
   _____ Y _____ N
6. Have your parents remarried? _____ Mom _____ Dad
7. Do you feel your parents might remarry? _____ each other _____ Mom may remarry another _____ Dad may remarry another.
8. Do you blame one or both parents for the divorce?
   _____ Both _____ Mom _____ Dad
9. Do you feel that you are to blame for your parents' divorce?
   _____ Yes _____ No
10. Do you think you were partially to blame for your parents' divorce?
    _____ Yes _____ No
11. Do you dream about your parents getting remarried or back together again?
    _____ Yes _____ No
12. Do you want to know more about the divorce? _____ Yes _____ No
13. Do you feel angry about the divorce? _____ Yes _____ No
14. Do you feel you can talk to your Mom about the divorce?
    _____ Yes _____ No
    Can you talk to your Dad? _____ Yes _____ No
15. How do you feel about your parents' dating someone else?
    _____ good _____ bad _____ angry _____ happy _____ sad
16. Do you often feel lonely? _____ Yes _____ No
17. If you are living with your Mom, do you feel you can call your Dad whenever you want? _____ Yes _____ No
18. If you live with your Dad, do you feel you can call your Mom whenever you want? _____ Yes _____ No
19. Do you think your Mom knows how you feel about her divorce?
    _____ Yes _____ No
20. Do you think your Dad knows how you feel about his divorce?
    _____ Yes _____ No
21. Have you ever talked to a friend about your parents' divorce?
    _____ Yes _____ No
22. Do other kids seem to understand how you feel about your parents' divorce?
    _____ Yes _____ No

23. Do you feel teachers understand how your parents' divorce affects you?
 _____ Yes _____ No _____ Some do
24. Are you able to talk to a teacher about your parents' divorce?
 _____ Yes _____ No
25. Does the divorce make it difficult to concentrate at school?
 _____ Yes _____ No
26. Would you like to see the parent you are *not* living with more often?
 _____ Yes _____ No
27. Would you like to have the counselor talk with your parent about any of these answers? _____ Yes _____ No
 _____ Only the ones I have marked with an "X."
28. If you marked "Yes" or "X" in the above item, would you want to be present when the counselor talks with your parent? _____ Yes _____ No

Appendix 5-2

FEELING VOCABULARY

(Adapted from Allers, 1982)

AFRAID	WEAK	STRONG
alarmed	ashamed	accomplished
anxious	beaten	aware
apprehensive	boxed in	brave
chicken	crazy	capable
cornered	defenseless	competent
cowardly	despondent	eager
desperate	doomed	energetic
fearful	exhausted	firm
fidgety	faint	forceful
frightened	fallen apart	important
jittery	frail	open
jumpy	helpless	responsible
nervous	inadequate	robust
overwhelmed	powerless	safe
panicky	relaxed	smart
pressured	shaken	steadfast
scared	shaky	together
shaky	shattered	trustful
tense	strengthless	valuable
terrified	weakened	vigorous

Appendix 5-2 (Continued)

FEELING VOCABULARY

(Adapted from Allers, 1982)

HAPPY	SAD	LOVING	ANGRY
alive	bothered	accepting	aggravated
beautiful	burdened	admiring	betrayed
bubbly	dejected	appreciative	bitter
comfortable	depressed	caring	bugged
content	despairing	close	burned
enthusiastic	despondent	concerned	cheated
excited	different	desirous	crabby
fantastic	disappointed	devoted	disgusted
fortunate	discouraged	fond	dissatisfied
friendly	disillusioned	friendly	disturbed
glowing	down	generous	edgy
good	downcast	giving	frustrated
groovy	empty	human	furious
lively	gloomy	intimate	grouchy
overjoyed	hurt	likeable	hateful
peaceful	left out	patient	impatient
pleased	low	respectful	irritable
satisfied	miserable	special	mad
terrific	sorrowful	tender	mean
thankful	unhappy	yearning	resentful

Appendix 5-3

EVALUATION OF SEMINAR EXPERIENCE

Please answer the following questions on your sheet of paper.

1. How did you feel when you entered this group? Use feeling vocabulary. ___
2. How do you feel about this group now? _____

3. Have you changed any attitudes since you entered this group? Explain. ___

4. Name one thing you have done in this group that makes you proud.

5. Did members of this group share their honest feelings with each other? Explain or give an example. ___

6. Did you feel that group members understood your feelings and supported you?
   Explain. _____

7. Did you learn from any other member's experiences how to cope with problems arising from the divorce of your parent?
   Explain. _____
   _____

Appendix 5-4

GROUP SEMINAR
FINAL EVALUATION

1. What were some benefits you received from our sessions? _____
   _____
   _____

2. What are some changes you would suggest for future seminars? _____
   _____
   _____

3. Would you suggest that your friends attend a similar seminar? _____

REFERENCES

Allers, Robert D.: *Divorce, Children, and the School.* Princeton, Princeton Book, 1982.

Elkind, David: *All Grown Up & No Place To Go: Teen-agers in Crisis.* Menlo Park, Addison-Wesley, 1984.

Glick, Paul & Norton, Arthur: *American Demographic.* 1979. In Peters, 1985.

Green, B. J.: Helping children of divorce: A multimodal approach. *Elementary School Guidance and Counseling, 13:*31–45, October 1978.

Hammatt-Kavaloski, Jane: Family change: A challenge to school social workers, *Social Work in Education, 4:*35–46, 1982.

Peters, Lori J.: Teens of divorce: Group counseling in the schools. *CAPS Capsule.* Educational Resources Information Center/Counseling and Personnel Services, (2), 1985.

Richards, A. & Willis, I.: *How to Get It Together When Your Parents Are Coming Apart.* New York, McKay, 1976.

Sheridan, John T., Baker, Stanley B., and de Lissovoy, Vladimir: Structured group counseling and explicit bibliotherapy as in-school strategies for preventing problems in youth of changing families. *The School Counselor.* 32 (2):134–141, November 1984.

Nonprint Media

Sunburst Communications. Redefining the family Part I; Single-parent families Part II; Stepparents and blended families Part III. *Coping with Family Changes.* [Filmstrip with cassettes]. Sunburst Communications, 1983.

Chapter Six

WRITE FOR SELF-UNDERSTANDING

WRITE A COLLEGE APPLICATION ESSAY

RUTH PERLSTEIN

Rationale

Entire families become stressed at college application time. As a high school counselor for twenty years, I have observed that writing the application essay is the ultimate stressor in the college application process, particularly for the student aspiring to attend a selective college. For this student, the essay might make a difference, but the student often procrastinates, convinced that he/she has nothing to say.

Most college applications require variations on personal statements. The basic question is: "Where have you been for the last seventeen years?" Sadly, the reluctant writer is thinking, "Nowhere."

High school counselors have worthy goals for students: self-exploration, self-concept enhancement, and decision-making. Since these goals can be realized through deciding what to write about oneself and how to revise that writing, helping students produce college application essays is an appropriate counseling activity.

Books with advice for the writer and samples of essays that have worked flood the market. Although modeling appears neither useful nor appropriate, free writing, letting thoughts flow on paper without critical judgment, offers a powerful opportunity for student self-exploration and expression. Don Murray (1984) advocates free writing, and in his book, *Intensive Journal Therapy,* Ira Progoff (1975) shows how free writing develops increased self-knowledge.

The underlying fear of self-disclosure in writing probably is the fear that others will judge, laugh at, or reject the feelings the writer has dared to expose. Responding as an audience to writing not only facilitates revision, but acknowledges the work and value of the individual writer (Mohr, 1984).

Response to an audience is helpful because it offers acceptance, encouragement, reality checking, and affirmation of worth of the writer, in addition to suggestions to improve one's statement about oneself. It is important that the writer read his work aloud to the listener because reading aloud helps determine voice, a crucial element in a good personal essay. A Yale admissions counselor commented (Winerip, 1984) that although she reads thousands of applications each year, only about five a year are "so natural, and so clearly from the heart, so naive, and so unsophisticated," that they cause her to stop, and "examine the file more carefully."

Leading groups to help students deal with the college application process is crucial for several reasons. First, no counselor has time to help students individually produce these essays. Second, the students function as a counseling group, acknowledging, encouraging, reality checking, and building trust in each other. In addition, the writer gets practice in eliciting audience response not unlike the response of admissions committee members.

Parents often complain that their children procrastinate in writing their essays, but parental nagging fails to help. Tension in families seems to increase at college application time. Sometimes, in desperation, parents actually try to write the essays. This attempt not only is patently unethical, but is not helpful because parents and students have different voices, which can easily be detected. College admissions counselors usually can distinguish the writing of high school students from the writing of adults. These admissions counselors also are naturally suspicious of applicants with brilliant essays but low verbal test scores. In addition, too much intrusion by parents can be demoralizing to a child. Presenting this process to family groups, the counselor helps bridge parent-child communication, and coaches parents to encourage their children through a positive approach. Family workshops help parents to separate from their children by seeing them as worthwhile, capable, and responsible.

Description of the Groups

The counselor can use the basic model or adapt it in various ways. This model includes: (1) a classroom presentation to juniors or seniors, (2) an introductory session for parents, (3) a group session for families, inviting students with their parents, and (4) small, informal student groups of three to six sessions. All sessions take approximately fifty minutes.

The classroom presentation to juniors or seniors takes one classroom period. The group session for parents introduces the process and the family session of two or more families works particularly well for seniors and their parents. Three to fifteen students can meet for the small, informal student groups. The introductory workshops introduce the students and their families to the series of small group workshops and motivate students to join the series of group sessions.

Goals

The primary goal of this group is for members to write at least one draft of a college application essay about themselves. The classroom presentation is primarily motivational and instructional. It de-mystifies the process of writing the application essay. In this presentation the counselor attempts to help students affirm their worth as interesting people and as writers. The objective of the classroom group session is to motivate students to think ahead, and get started in writing the essay. Hopefully, they will develop greater self-knowledge, and understand the writing process.

The objective of the session for parents is to de-mystify the process for parents. It is to help parents encourage, but not tamper with their child's essay. Family groups learn how to improve communication, to give, and accept support.

Finally, the small, informal student groups function as support groups, giving feedback and encouragement to members to continue working through the writing process.

Procedures

The introductory large group presentation begins with the counselor asking students to write five minute jot lists of things they like to do, things they do well, and things they are proud of. The counselor circulates as students write, encouraging students to brainstorm quickly, and record items the counselor sees on the various lists. After five minutes, the counselor shares some random observations. The counselor might say:

> What a group! Here are writers, athletes, musicians, shoppers, chess players, readers, observers, collectors, organizers, hikers, artists, and

cooks. Richard Moll, author of many books on college admission said, 'Every person who has passed through the teen-age years has something worthwhile to say . . . and we admissions counselors listen' (1980).

At this point, students begin to look more confident. Each student is beginning to feel a little better about him/her-self. Each has taken a risk by jotting something down and survived the counselor's eavesdropping. When the counselor refers to items on his/her list positively and anonymously, the student affirms his/her self-worth. After sharing the list, the counselor might share some observations about connections on the lists. One student in a group might list the following: math team, chess, chem lab, thinking, walking, camp, labs. The counselor might comment that this student likes to solve problems. Students find unusual connections that eventually produce good ideas for essays. For example, one student listed: Teen Democratic group, sailing, books. Later he wrote an essay indicating how Buckley, a political conservative, really did have something to say to this political liberal by writing a book on sailing and speaking, "sailor to sailor."

In the large group, the counselor might suggest:

> Close your eyes and think about the items on your list and any connection that happens to come to you. Pianists . . . think about a moment when you were just about to perform . . . what do you see? What do you hear? What are you saying to yourself? Write about it . . . be specific. . . . Science students, recall a specific lab that intrigued you . . . , what was happening? . . . write. . . . Others relax, think about a specific time, a place, an experience . . . a small incident . . . write. . . . Readers and movie goers, think about a particular incident or character . . . write. . . .

As participants get ideas, they begin writing. Gradually all participants write. The counselor should allow about ten minutes for the free writing. Meanwhile, the counselor circulates, and helps writers who are stuck. One way to help reluctant writers is to comment on or ask about the jot list. For example, the problem solver who wrote about the math team, chess, thinking, etc. might be asked, "What does this say about you?" or "What would a friend say about this list?" The student might respond, "People always say, "Oh, Ann, you think too much!" At this point the counselor might say, "I like that. Write that down and keep going, Ann!"

The counselor might continue suggesting personal experiences to students. When the counselor notices that a student gets an idea, he/she can encourage the student to begin writing random thoughts.

Another approach is to hand a list of typical application questions to the student (Appendix 6-4), and ask him/her to choose one. Another alternative is to give the student a different list of topics. The handout entitled "Study Skills Journals" (Appendix 6-3), provides useful topics for self-exploration that can yield good beginnings for personal essays. If the counselor continues to encourage students they will participate.

After the ten minute writing activity, the counselor assigns dyads or small groups for a structured exercise. The counselor distributes a handout with revision questions (Appendix 6-1), and instructs each writer to read his writing aloud to his partner. After he/she reads the writing aloud, the writer asks the following questions of the listener: "What do you like about my draft? Is there a line or section that grabs you? Is there a possible lead? What do you want to know more about? Does a real person emerge?"

During this activity, which takes about ten to fifteen minutes, the counselor circulates to keep the group members on task. The counselor can briefly join dyads or small groups, listening and responding, and asking volunteers to share their writing with the large group. In this way, members always volunteer, and no one is embarrassed. In dyads or small groups, volunteering to read aloud is not threatening.

After each group member has read and received responses to his/her questions, volunteers read to the large group. Then group members respond. At this point, it is useful to tie the exercise to research on the college application essay.

The following quotes from admissions personnel might be posted and discussed.

- "If it comes out of you, then it's good . . . the lead off sentence is important" (Brown University, Shore, 1979).
- "Things that are fake go clank" (Harvard, Moll, 1980).
- "Be thoughtful, and thought provoking, not cute or vacuous" (Princeton, Wickendon, 1979).

Students can discuss possible leads and whether real persons emerge. They should discuss voice, and the counselor might explain that voice is best heard when the reader reads aloud. At this point samples might be read to illustrate the posted comments.

It is useful to compare essays on like topics. For example, two different essays were submitted to answer the same question, "Describe a person who has influenced you" (Appendix 6-2). Obviously, the second essay not only has a more distinct voice, but says more about the writer. What the writer says in any given writing needs to be addressed in group sessions or in workshops. Samples and discussions of essays are good transition points in the workshops. These discussions might conclude an introductory workshop, or begin a second session on revising the essay.

When the counselor follows the basic model described above and conducts the meeting for parents, the counselor may encourage the parents to write. Writing helps parents understand the stress their child is experiencing. Parents also learn that their writing does not sound like that of their children. Their son or daughter's voice, not the parent's voice, is appropriate in the essay. Parents begin to learn that they can be supportive, but they cannot write for their child.

The same model can also be used in groups of families. Sometimes in small groups comprised of family groups, the counselor instructs students only to write, asking parents to peruse literature on the college application essay (Appendix 6-5 and Bibliography) while their child writes.

In the family workshop, students read aloud to their parents, and ask the designated questions from the reader response sheet (Appendix 6-1). In this way, students share their thoughts with their parents, and the parents listen and respond positively. Not only does this exercise teach parents good listening skills to encourage their children to write, but it creates a situation where parents praise and positively reinforce their child. As an exercise to facilitate good family communication and positive sharing, it is useful. Families leave these workshops smiling and feeling comfortable with one another.

The series of small counseling groups provides time to motivate students to write. The series also provides an opportunity for students to learn more about themselves.

Session 1

Procedures: Ask students to write jot lists, using the same directions given above. Then ask volunteers to read their lists aloud. The following is a typical sample list:

Like: hiking, reading, football, camping, baseball, movies.

Do Well: write term papers, science labs, campfires.
Proud of: science fair project, scout badge, butterfly collection.

Ask students to help the volunteer explore "what this list says about you." Encourage students to explore connections on the list, and brainstorm suggestions for beginning free writing that can lead to a personal statement.

Commentary:

Some group members might comment that this student loves the outdoors. Another might point out that he/she enjoys reading about nature, and researched a related topic for a science fair project. The counselor or a group member may probe further, asking, "How did you get involved in your science fair topic?" "What kind of nature books do you read?" "Why do you like a particular author?" Group members can take turns asking questions of members, sharing lists until participants appear to develop insight.

The counselor can suggest that each member think about a moment in his/her experience or explore the connections of the jot list, and free write, trying to be as specific as possible. Students focus on what they see, think, feel, and sense.

After students write for ten minutes, some members may volunteer to read to the large group. If not, members may share their writing with partners, and ask revision questions. After the partner has finished reading, the writer asks, "What do you like?" "What do you want to know more about?" "Does a real person emerge?"

These questions promote readers to give positive feedback to writers. Memorable lines emerge. Lines like, "I have a love-hate relationship with my clock," and "At five I was shaking hands and meeting my public" make good essay beginnings. Members often encourage each other to continue free writing after the session.

To summarize, the counselor asks participants if they feel ready to write. If so, they should describe how they will continue exploratory writing.

Session 2

Procedures: Use a different approach to encourage self-discovery and motivate students to produce detailed free writing. Conduct this session using guided imagery.

Relax, close your eyes, and think about some of the events in your life so far. Try to note periods of time that stand out. When did a specific time period begin? When did it end? As you think about experiences and time periods, jot them down. Place them in chronological order, beginning with birth. If you prefer, think about specific experiences or themes such as activities or your family.

Commentary:

An addicted Boston Red Sox fan, zeroed in on a moment in a period of his development as a baseball fan, cited other experiences from other periods, and demonstrated insight, enthusiasm, and humor. Another student wrote about her passion for philosophical ideas, and supported this with wonderful anecdotes after thinking about books she read during recent periods on her list.

A session devoted to creating milestones and sharing them can result in increased self-knowledge and many new ideas for writing. In this session, as in others, it is important to respect privacy, and request volunteers for sharing rather than requiring all group members to share.

After volunteers share milestones, students may share application questions, and discuss how these questions relate to some of their milestones. Students will notice that most of the questions really do ask about significant events and people. Even specific questions like "Describe a person, living or dead, you would like to invite to dinner" are more easily answered when lists of heroes are generated through a milestone list or after values are clarified by focusing on the milestone list. This list is not intended to serve as an outline, but rather to suggest ideas, and to help the writer become organized. Many different lists may be used.

Next, volunteers read aloud to the group. Again, group members respond to the questions, "What do you like?" "What do you want to know more about?" "Does a real person emerge?" If subdivided into smaller groups, the counselor can circulate from group to group.

At the conclusion of the session, the counselor asks whether students feel they are ready to write their drafts. They state their goals for writing between sessions, and agree to bring questions and drafts to the next session.

Session 3

This session focuses on revision. Readers share with dyad partners or with the large group by reading their questions and their drafts aloud, and asking questions. If the group has more than six members, the counselor subdivides the group. The counselor distributes the revision sheet (Appendix 6-1) and after the writer asks the questions, the group members respond. "What does this writing say about me?" "Considering the question, is this answer appropriate?" "How might I develop my ideas further?" "What forms might I use?"

A student who wrote a poetic essay describing how "glasses clinked and time mellowed out" realized that his essay showed how he wished to escape from reality, and acknowledged that this is not what he wanted to say about himself to an admissions committee. Another student explored ways of showing her growth as a journalist, and elicited feedback from the group about various ways to develop her ideas. After positive feedback from the group, she decided to write an essay in the form of an interview.

To conclude the session, students describe how they feel about their writing, what they have learned about themselves, and state their plans for writing to prepare for the next session.

Session 4

Procedures: Post or distribute a new list of questions. Begin with the same key questions, but focus on organization and clarity. "What does the writing say?" "Is this thoughtful and interesting?" "Is the focus clear?" "Do anecdotes support what the essay says?" "Are any parts unclear?" "Are any parts unrelated to the main idea?" "Is the essay organized logically?" "Are the transitions smooth?" "Does the beginning grab the reader?" "Does the ending sound appropriate?"

Commentary:

Volunteers read drafts, and group members respond to each draft by answering the questions for the writer. During this session, failure to use anecdotal detail becomes obvious. Group members encourage appropriate revision by asking questions. For example, students might ask a dancer who wrote a bland draft about dancing, "What is it about a particular dance that makes it challenging?" "What are examples of specific ideas you express in dance?" "How do you go about expressing that specific idea through dance?" "What do some of the routines look like or sound like?"

During this session, writers often have difficulty deleting material from their drafts. Group members can ask how sections relate to main ideas. In this way, the writer can more easily let go of irrelevant portions of their drafts. One student really wanted to use a paragraph about her student government experience, but it had absolutely nothing to do with her topic, the closeness of her family. Finally she was able to delete her paragraph, and more effectively organize her statement.

To conclude this session, students share their feelings, insights, and goals.

Session 5

Procedure: This final session is similar to the previous session. Students find several revision sessions are helpful before they are ready to edit and proof their essays.

Commentary:

Some students can begin proofing during this session. These students can read their work aloud, and ask for feedback about wordiness, areas that don't sound smooth, and word choice. Group members point out problem areas needing editing, but they do not rewrite sentences. It is unethical for others to write sentences, and often it distorts the writer's voice.

Reviewing mechanical errors is not included in the workshop, but students must understand that the final step in writing is editing and proofreading. The basic model in both small and large groups involves writing, reading aloud, seeking feedback, and revising. This model focuses on self-discovery and development of the ability to express that discovery in writing. Group members practice listening, encouraging, writing, and revising. These skills will promote personal growth as well as good college application essays.

Evaluation

The purpose of these workshops is for students to acknowledge that they do have something worthwhile to say about themselves, and to free them to say it in a personal way. By completing this questionnaire we can learn if we accomplished this purpose.

Directions: Please complete the following questions to determine if the purpose was met in this series of workshops.

1. Did participating in these workshops help you learn more about yourself? If so, what did you learn, and how? I learned that I ___
   _____

2. Did you change your feeling about yourself in any way as a result of these workshops? I changed _____
   _____

3. Do you feel more capable of writing a good application essay as a result of this workshop? I improved my writing when _____
   _____
   _____

Appendix 6-1

THE APPLICATION ESSAY, A PROCESS

- **Writer Free Writes.**
- **Writer Seeks a Response to His/Her Writing.**

Writer reads his/her essay aloud and asks the listener the following questions about the essay.

1. What do you like about my draft?
2. Is there a possible lead for a personal statement/essay? If so, what? (circle or underline).
3. What do you want to know more about?
4. Does a real person emerge?

- **Writer Revises.**

Writer asks the following questions:

1. What does this writing say about me?
2. Is what it says appropriate? (Does the draft answer the question, present me well, speak appropriately to the audience?)
3. What else, if anything, can I say to support what I am saying?
4. What forms can I use to say what I have decided to say?

- **Writer Revises.**

  Writer checks organization and clarity.

- **Writer Edits.**

  Writer checks grammar, punctuation, and spelling.

Appendix 6-2

TWO ESSAYS ANSWERING THE SAME QUESTION TWO GRANDPARENTS

Question: Please describe a single event or person who has had a significant impact on your life to date.

Essay Number One:

I have found that the death of my Grandmother has had a significant impact on my life. It brought me next to reality and I was given a new outlook on life. It drove home the fact that no one is perfect for we all have that fatal flaw. It caused me to look to my future and make a decision as to what I shall do with myself. At this moment I am pursuing a goal which I have set. That goal is what I came up with after my Grandmother's death and I shall pursue it to the best of my ability and college is a major step toward my goal (Ripple, 1986, p. 23).

Essay Number Two:

My grandfather died suddenly and unexpectedly of a heart attack last year while I was away at school. He was big, rough, and strong smelling, like a stale airport lounge. He was my mother's father; she hated his roughness, his Brooklyn accent, his table manners. I didn't know what she was talking about. I just knew that he was always swooping me up into the air, forming an arc with me, saying as he did so, 'Light as a feather.'....

He took me everywhere and made me promise not to tell. To the off-track betting parlor where men who smelled far worse than my grandfather pinched my cheeks and told me never to gamble. He taught me how to spit off the Brooklyn Bridge. "A good strong spit," he called it, "not a shitspit."

My mother sensed all of these things, but I never told. My grandfather knew this and liked me even better, took me to even more places with him. He let me drop slugs into the baskets at the toll booths. He showed me the factory in downtown Brooklyn where he had once gotten into a fight and knocked a man's teeth out....

I didn't know that my grandfather, a retired fireman, didn't have enough money, that secretly my parents gave my grandmother money to pay some bills. When my grandfather found out, he stormed out of the house and didn't come back until he had found a job driving taxicabs. He told me about his new job and what he said to his boss. 'Look, I don't drive no cabs on Saturday mornings, you got that straight, cause I got a regular date with the most beautiful broad in the world, and I ain't gonna stand her up.' I giggled with delight; my mother, an English teacher and a feminist, groaned.

One Saturday morning we arrive as usual, my mother about to just let me out of the car and head back home again. But my grandmother came out into the driveway and told me to get back in the car, grandpa was sick.... He just wanted my mother to get me out of the house, to keep me from learning that he had been mugged the night before while driving his cab (Ripple, 1986, p. 24).

Appendix 6-3

STUDY SKILLS JOURNAL ENTRIES

1. Memory
   Dialogue with your memory. First, list its characteristics.
   Describe your feelings about your memory. What factors contribute to your remembering? Recall a time when you felt particularly good about your memory. Describe how you can best use your memory.

2. Test Feedback
   Describe what was happening when you were taking a specific test. How did you feel? Describe your thoughts as you attempted to answer a difficult question. Now that you review your feelings about the test, how could you have approached the test item differently?
   Dialogue with your teacher about a specific test item.

3. Procrastination
   Recall your earliest experience with procrastination. What was happening? What were you doing? How were you feeling? Focus on that situation. What does it tell you about yourself? Describe a time when you actually used a time schedule. Describe your feelings about the schedule.
   Recall a time you succeeded in avoiding procrastination. Describe what was happening and how you felt.
   Dialogue with your calendar.

Appendix 6-4

APPLICATION ESSAY QUESTIONS

Brown University

"... Since our knowledge is limited to the information provided, why not then use this opportunity to tell us about anything you think we should know?"

Carleton College

"What do you see as the turning point(s) or important events in your life, and why do you view them as such?"

"Who are the people who have done the most to influence your personal development, and in what ways were they influential?"
"What have you learned from your extracurricular involvement?"
"Describe the social atmosphere at your school, and tell how you fit in it."
"What have you learned from your extracurricular involvement?"
"Describe the social atmosphere at your school, and tell how you fit in it."

Cornell University

"Write a short essay about an intellectual, social, political, or personal issue you feel is important. We are interested in your choice of topic as well as the quality of its presentation."

Duke University

"What is it that you do that best reflects your personality?"

Harvard University

"Briefly discuss a book that has made a great impact on you."

Massachusetts Institute of Technology

"What responsibility have you had for others and how has it affected your personal growth?"
"Make up a question, state it clearly, and answer it. Use your imagination, recognizing that those who read it will not mind being entertained."

University of Pennsylvania

"If you were given the opportunity to spend an evening with any one person, living, deceased, or fictional, whom would you choose and why?"
"If you had the power to eliminate one problem which exists in the world today, what would it be and why?"
"If you were given the opportunity to leave a time capsule for posterity in the cornerstone of your city hall, what one book, one mechanical object, and one other item of your choosing would you leave as a statement about life in the late twentieth century and why?"
"What is the best piece of advice you have ever received?"

Common Application Questions

"Evaluate a significant experience or achievement that has special meaning for you."
"Discuss some issue of personal, local, or national concern, and its importance to you."
"If you could travel through time, and interview a prominent figure in the arts, politics, religion, or science, for example, whom would you choose and why?"

Appendix 6-5

ADDITIONAL RESOURCES

Bauld, Harry: *On Writing the College Application Essay.* New York, Barnes & Noble, 1987.

Power, Helen W. and DiAntonio, Robert: *The Admissions Essay.* Secaucus, Lyle Stewart, 1987.

REFERENCES

McGinty, Sara Myers: Unpublished presentation, National Association of College Admissions Counselors (NACAC) conference, Washington, 1986.

Mohr, Marian M.: *Revision The Rhyme of Meaning.* Upper Montclair, Boynton/Cook, 1984.

Moll, Richard: *Playing the Private College Admissions Game.* New York, Penguin, 1980.

Murray, Donald: *Write to Learn.* New York, Holt, Rinehart & Winston, 1984.

Progoff, Ira: *Intensive Journal Therapy.* New York, Dialogue, 1975.

Ripple, G. Gary: The footwear of life and other stories: Stories from the teen scene. *William and Mary Alumnae Gazette Magazine. 54* (1), July-August 1986. pp. 23–24.

Ripple, G. Gary: *Do It — Write: How to Prepare a Great College Application.* Alexandria, Octameron, 1986.

Schwartz, Mimi: How to Write College Application Essays. *Princeton, Peterson Guides, 1982.*

Shore, Debra: "The agony and the ecstasy: An application to Brown," *Brown Alumni Monthly, 79:7, 26–32, 1979.*

Wickendon, James W.: *The Admissions Process at Selective Colleges.* Princeton, Peterson Guides, 1979.

Winerip, Michael: "Hot colleges," *New York Times Magazine,* pp. 68–173, November 18, 1984.

Chapter Seven

INCREASE CAREER AWARENESS

CAREER AWARENESS FOR HIGH SCHOOL FRESHMEN

Kenneth A. Gaudreault

Rationale

Today's youth must cope, not only with the anxieties inherent in adolescence, but also with a rapidly changing society, an unknown technology, and an unpredictable economy. In this unstable environment, young people are expected to make important decisions affecting their future. Students in the ninth grade, ages fourteen or fifteen are at a developmental stage when they want to learn more about themselves and need to consider appropriate options.

Ninth grade students have time to choose high school courses to prepare them for their desired future. Students are more serious in their studies when they see relevance to their learning and can relate this learning to their goals. Students with concrete academic goals are more apt to achieve them than students with no goals.

Recent national surveys indicate that career guidance is a major issue for American families. Parents report that helping their children choose a career is their second most pressing concern (Herbert 1987). In 1983, over 70 percent of eighth and eleventh grade students who were questioned, said they wanted more help with making career plans (Herbert 1987).

Recognizing the importance and influence of parents' involvement in career education, and desiring to elicit parents' contributions, parents are welcome to attend all sessions of this seminar. They are particularly invited to the first and last meetings which are held in the evening. During the first session, the parents are informed of the strong influence they have in their children's career decisions. The leader requests that the students discuss each session and each activity with their parents. This encourages student-parent communication and enables members to become aware of their own and their parents' perspectives.

During the last session, parents are provided a summary of the information that was taught in the seminar. Members discuss their current interests and their plans to learn more about these careers.

This seminar is designed to increase wise decision-making and career awareness. Members who have developed critical thinking, recognized the attributes and detriments of different careers, and compared specific careers with their desired life-styles, have skills that will help them in the future. They will have developed appropriate career goals compatible with their educational plans and life-style.

Goals

The seminar is planned so that each member will identify and integrate his/her feelings, interests, and values into a life plan. Two main goals for this seminar are that the members:

- Select three careers that interest them and indicate the factors about these careers that appeal to them. These factors should be consistent with what they have learned and stated about themselves (interests, likes and dislikes).
- Identify the necessary preparation to enter these careers (college, graduate school, on-the-job training, technical school, apprenticeship,) and indicate the reasons this preparation will help them compete and achieve their desired career goals.

Definition of the Seminar

The leader publicizes the seminar through the school newspaper, daily bulletin, parents' newsletter, flyers and posters in ninth grade classrooms. Counselors of ninth grade students inform freshmen of this opportunity. The leader selects members from different backgrounds with different career goals after individual screening of interested applicants (Appendix 1-5).

Members must agree to attend all eight sessions and practice the group rules. The first and last sessions are in the evening; the other six weekly sessions are rotated among the six periods to minimize absences from any one class. The leader gives the meeting schedule to teachers before the first session. The group meets in the school career center.

The counselor may use *Career Skills,* (Kelly and Volz-Patton, 1987) and

Student Activity Workbook: Career Skills, (Kelly and Volz-Patton, 1987) as an additional reference, or use these books in a follow-up group.

Group Rules

Members are to listen, attend to and respect others' ideas, comments, and opinions, and participate in the activities unless they "pass."

Sessions

Session 1

Members and Parents

Objectives for Members:
- Become acquainted with each other
- Abide by the group rules
- Express personal values in a concrete way

Procedure of the Leader:
1. Greet and introduce the members and parents. Invite the members to sit in an inner circle with the parents outside this circle. Tell the parents of their influence on their children's decisions of post-secondary education and career.
2. Introduce the members. Each member gives his/her name and a personal quality which he/she feels makes him/her different from the others. The leader summarizes by repeating each student's name and the quality stated.
3. Introduce the parents. Each parent does the same activity and the leader summarizes the parents' names and qualities stated.
4. Give all members a loose-leaf notebook in which they are to keep all papers about career decision making and all papers provided in this group. This is their career packet.
5. Distribute and review the group rules.
6. Promote career-awareness. Ask parents to introduce themselves again, this time stating their current career, and the educational preparation and job experience that is necessary to succeed in their career.
7. Ask parents to list three attributes and three negative aspects of

their current career. Discuss. Invite the members to ask relevant questions.
8. Ask parents to identify the personal traits, abilities, and goals that (1) are essential and (2) lead to success in their career. Discuss.
9. Provide an opportunity for students who are interested in the careers of the parents who are attending to discuss the above later.
10. Promote self-awareness. Before young people can make realistic career decisions for the future, they need to be aware of their current likes, dislikes, and goals. Ask members to complete "My Personal Traits" (Appendix 7-1). Explain the directions and how the results will be used.
11. Suggest that members discuss their answers to "My Personal Traits" with their parents. If parents are not present, discuss their answers with another student.
12. Bring the group together. Summarize by explaining the self-awareness task and the need to clarify goals before making career decisions.
13. Ask members and their parents if they have any questions about the process that will be used in this group. Answer questions.
14. Ask members and parents to complete the "Group Feedback Form" (Appendix 2-3).
15. Invite parents to future sessions. Give the dates of all sessions to members and parents.

Session 2

Objectives for Members:

- Become aware of preferred life-styles and values.

As group members become aware of their individual values, they also become aware of their preferred life-style. This "Values Auction" helps students learn their preferred life-styles as they refine and test their current values to learn what they prize most.

Procedure of the Leader:

1. Distribute the "Values Auction Worksheets" (Appendix 7-2). Explain the concept of life units as used in this activity.
2. Remind members to think about each item and be honest in their choices.

3. Conduct a values auction by giving each member one hundred units and asking them to bid with no bids smaller than a unit of five. The highest bid wins that item. The leader is the auctioneer.
4. Suggest that members keep track of their bids and the sales on their auction worksheets, and remind them to include these in their career packets.
5. Divide the group into sub-groups of three, with one member designated as the recorder. The recorder lists the names and highest bids of the three. Each member tells the other members of the triad how the value for which he/she bid a high number reflects his/her priorities in life. Other triad members ask questions about decisions that the member has made that are consistent or inconsistent with the value that he/she desired to purchase.
6. Reassemble the large group and ask the recorders to summarize.
7. Ask the members if they learned anything about themselves from the activity. Distribute the "I Learned Statements" (Appendix 7-3) and ask members to complete them.
8. Assign the "Work Ethic Worksheet" (Appendix 7-4) as homework. Ask members to discuss this worksheet with their parents and then bring this completed worksheet to the next session.
9. Remind members of the date and time for the next session.

Session 3

Objectives for Members:

- Acquire knowledge of educational and occupational paths.
- Begin to plan appropriate post-secondary education and vocations.

Procedure of the Leader:

1. Explain that individuals may feel differently about the work ethic. Ask volunteers to tell how they answered the items on their completed "Work Ethic Sheet" (Appendix 7-4).
2. Introduce the two worksheets entitled "Educational Training Levels" (Appendix 7-5), and "School Subjects and Careers" (Appendix 7-6), by telling members that the level of success that a student has in high school courses can provide clues as to future success in occupations that are related to that subject. For example, a person who experiences high achievement in the language arts, espe-

cially in writing, might consider a career as a reporter, technical writer or editor. Suggest that students also consider the comfort or ease with which they work on the subject, and the personal enjoyment that they experience from studying that subject.
3. Divide the group into triads.
4. Distribute one copy of the first worksheet, "Educational Training Levels" (Appendix 7-5) to each triad. Members work together to complete this worksheet. Explain the directions and give them ample time to complete the task.
5. Assemble the entire group and ask one member from each triad to respond to the items. Ask members: "What were the most difficult items to complete?" "Why?" "What items were the easiest to complete?" "Why?" "Which items had the most alternatives?" "Why?"
6. Summarize the session. Ask members to think about different occupational settings for next session. They may use references in the career center or may interview people to add more careers to their lists.

Session 4

Objectives for Members:

- Increase knowledge about work settings.
- Increase knowledge about educational requirements for specific careers.

Procedure of the Leader:

1. Introduce work settings by pointing out that members can narrow their interests to one or two clusters and not make a specific career choice too soon. Give examples of how their decision of what they do after high school, or which college they may choose to attend, may depend upon their choice of career cluster.
2. Ask members to work in triads. Distribute worksheets "Career Settings" (Appendix 7-7) to each triad. After members have completed the worksheet, discuss answers. Ask questions such as: "How much do you know about the careers you listed?" "Where did/can you get this information?" "How can you learn more about these careers?" "How many of you listed the career of one of your parents?" "How many of you listed the career of one of the

parents of a student in your triad?" "Do careers influence the friends you make?" "Have your parents' careers influenced the friends they have?" "Are there apparent reasons that people who work together enjoy a social life together?"
3. Summarize the session or ask a member to summarize what he/she learned from this session.

Session 5

Objectives for Members:

- Realize that each person is unique.
- Realize that choices are unique.
- Distinguish among interests, aptitudes, and abilities.
- Realize that career choices depend on individual interests, aptitudes, and abilities.

Procedure of the Leader:

1. Explain that career success depends on a combination of all three factors; interests, aptitudes, and abilities.
2. Distinguish among interests, aptitudes, and abilities by defining each:

   Interest — If you like what you are doing, then you don't mind doing it, regardless of the work or time involved. For instance, if you like repairing your car or cooking a meal, time flies while you are doing it. The same tasks are boring or tiring for others who have little interest in these jobs.

   Aptitude — Some people excel in certain areas of mathematics or mechanics and find them easy. Everyone has some high, average, and low aptitude for different tasks.

   Ability — Ability is usually measured by tests. Ability to learn is one factor in success.

3. Divide the group into new triads so members work with members they have not worked with before. Explain that each person will appraise his/her own interests. Distribute the "Appraisal of My Interests" (Appendix 7-8). Ask students to complete and then to discuss their interests in their triad. After all have finished, ask these questions: "Do you see any pattern to your likes and dislikes?" "How can understanding your likes and dislikes help you to select a career?" "Circle the things you particularly like."

4. Follow the same procedure with the "Appraisal of My Aptitude" (Appendix 7-9). Ask members: "Which are your strongest areas? Put an asterisk in front of these." "Which are your weakest areas? Put a minus in front of these." "How can this knowledge help you choose a career?"
5. Follow the same procedure with the "Appraisal of My Abilities" (Appendix 7-10). Discuss: "Do your grades predict your success in a career?" "Put an asterisk in front of the subjects in which you do particularly well." "Can you see any patterns to your strengths?" "Review your interests, aptitudes, and abilities."
6. Distribute the final assignment to take home to complete. Encourage members to discuss their autobiographies (Appendix 7-11) with their parents.

Session 6

Objectives for Members:

- Learn more about self.
- Learn how career interests reflect self.

Procedure of the Leader:

1. Select one interest inventory that is most appropriate for each member. Select from: Job-O, Self-Directed Search, Job Finding Map, COPS, COPS II, Differential Aptitude Test, or Harrington O'Shea.
2. Explain to members the reason different inventories are appropriate for different students.
3. Distribute the interest inventories and explain the directions. Students complete the surveys.
4. Explain the self-scoring process and the meaning of the career clusters.
5. Ask members to discuss what they learned from taking the survey. Stress that the results from one survey cannot determine what a person "should do." This is just one more item of information to include in the members' career packets.

Session 7

Objectives for Members:

- Use resources within the career center.
- Feel closure of the group.
- Help each other find resources.

Procedure of the Leader:

1. Review and tie together the concepts presented in this and previous sessions.
2. Review the location of all resources within the career center. Demonstrate the use of the media available and show the location of the printed materials.
3. Ask members to use the resources in the career center during this session to learn one new thing about a career cluster that is appropriate for them. At the end of the session, ask members to identify the career cluster they selected, and one new thing they learned during this session.
4. Ask members to identify the career interests of all other members, and indicate where other members can get more information. Ask if they know any adult who may help another member.
5. Encourage members to help each other, and to serve as resources to help each other in the future.
6. Recommend that members keep their career packets up-to-date in a place where they are easily retrieved.

Session 8

Members and Parents

Objectives for Parents:

- Be informed of the career decision-making process.
- Help sons/daughters continue the process of career decision-making.

Objectives for Members and Parents:

- Communicate and learn more about the careers the members find interesting and appropriate.
- Evaluate the group experience.

Procedure of the Leader:

1. Ask students in turn to review their unique interests, aptitudes, abilities, selected career, and something they learned about that career through their research.
2. Ask parents to contribute any knowledge, experience, or resource that may be helpful to any member.
3. Ask parents and students to complete the evaluation forms (Appendix 7-12).
4. Ask members and parents to discuss the value of this group, and make suggestions to improve the plan for the group.

Appendix 7-1

MY PERSONAL TRAITS

Last Name,	First, M.I.	Class of	Date

Last Name (Parent) First
Circle number of children in your family: 1 2 3 4 5 6 7 8 9
Check your position in your family.
Circle the answer that describes you.

1. I like to be with people.	Yes	No	Don't know
2. I get upset easily.	Yes	No	Don't know
3. I worry a lot.	Yes	No	Don't know
4. I am patient.	Yes	No	Don't know
5. I'm usually considerate of others.	Yes	No	Don't know
6. I like to plan school activities.	Yes	No	Don't know
7. I lack confidence in myself.	Yes	No	Don't know
8. I like to read.	Yes	No	Don't know
9. I like to speak to groups.	Yes	No	Don't know
10. I like to work with my hands.	Yes	No	Don't know
11. I am dependable.	Yes	No	Don't know
12. I have a sense of humor.	Yes	No	Don't know
13. I like to be outdoors.	Yes	No	Don't know

My Abilities   H = High   A = Average   L = Low

1. Art	H A L	6. Public Speaking	H A L
2. Athletics	H A L	7. Science	H A L
3. Drama	H A L	8. Selling	H A L
4. Mechanical	H A L	9. _____	H A L
5. Music	H A L	10. _____	H A L

My Post Secondary Plans

1. _____
2. _____

My Interests

1. _____
2. _____

My Part Time Work

1. _____
2. _____

My Goals Number your 1st, 2nd and 3rd choices in *each* column.

Long Range Goals	*Short Range Goals*
Adventure	Academic Success
Fame	Acceptance by Peers
Happy Marriage	Acceptance by Parents
Good Health	Acceptance by Teachers
Interesting Career	Active Social Life
Material Success	Athletic Success
Maximum Use of Abilities	Attractive Appearance
Prestige	Independence from Parents
Security	Many Clothes
Service to Society	Popularity with Friends
Travel	Other (Please list)

Appendix 7-2

VALUES AUCTION WORKSHEET

Adapted from James D. McHolland
Reprinted by Permission

LIFE UNITS I WANT TO SPEND	LIFE UNITS I BID	TOP BID	LIFE UNITS I SPENT
Being known as an honest person.			
Being known as a "fun" person.			

	LIFE UNITS I WANT TO SPEND	LIFE UNITS I BID	TOP BID	LIFE UNITS I SPENT
Having self-confidence & personal growth.				
Enjoying nature & beauty (any form).				
Having a life with meaning, purpose and fulfillment.				
Continuing to learn & gain knowledge.				
Helping the sick & disadvantaged.				
Having a physical appearance I can be proud of.				
Having honest, close friendships.				
Having a long and healthy life.				
Having a meaningful relationship with God.				
Having a good marriage relationship.				
Realizing satisfaction and success in the career/job of my choice.				
Assuring an equal opportunity for all people				
Having freedom to live my life as I want.				

	LIFE UNITS I WANT TO SPEND	LIFE UNITS I BID	TOP BID	LIFE UNITS I SPENT
Living a financially comfortable life.				
Accomplishing something worthwhile.				
Having a secure and positive family life.				
Enjoying an enjoyable, leisurely life.				
Enjoying unlimited travel, fine foods, recreational & cultural opportunities.				
Being a change agent.				
Enjoying a beautiful home in the setting of my choice.				
Developing my creativity and potential in any area.				
Owning a possession of great value.				

Appendix 7-3

I LEARNED STATEMENTS

Name _____ Date _____ Session _____

1. I learned that I _____

2. I realized that I _____

3. I relearned that I _____

4. I noticed that I _____

5. I discovered that I _____

6. I was surprised that I _____

7. I was disappointed that I _____

8. I was pleased that I _____

Appendix 7-4

THE IMPORTANCE OF WORK—THE WORK ETHIC

The work ethic is made up of the following VALUES:
1. Hard work is noble and necessary.
2. All honest work is dignified.
3. One achieves and succeeds through hard work and effort.
4. Any job, regardless of the task, is important and worthy of doing well. ("Any job worth doing, is worth doing right.")
5. Everyone should pull his/her own weight, earn his/her own way.

Discuss the above values with your parents. Ask what answers they may give to the questions below.

To help determine your own values regarding work, answer the following questions:

1. Do you think hard work is the key to success?
   _____ Yes, _____ No. Explain _____

2. Is there any kind of honest work that you wouldn't do? If so, name it. _____

3. Is American society too materialistic? Explain _____

   Are you more or less materialistic than your parents? _____
4. Do you think work is important for a full and satisfying life? _____
   Explain _____
5. Would you work if you didn't have to? _____

6. Can you think of jobs that no one would find satisfying and rewarding? If so, what jobs?

Appendix 7-5

EDUCATIONAL TRAINING LEVELS

Listed below are a number of levels of education or training. Your task is to identify four occupations that people can enter with that particular education or training.

High School (Diploma)
1. _____ 3. _____
2. _____ 4. _____

High School (Vocational/Technical emphasis)
1. _____ 3. _____
2. _____ 4. _____

On-The-Job Training (Provided by employer)
1. _____ 3. _____
2. _____ 4. _____

Apprenticeship Training
1. _____ 3. _____
2. _____ 4. _____

Special Career Training (Trade/Technical or Business school after completion of high school diploma).
1. _____ 3. _____
2. _____ 4. _____

Military Service
1. _____ 3. _____
2. _____ 4. _____

Community College (2 year, Associate Degree).
1. _____ 3. _____
2. _____ 4. _____

College or University (4 year, B.A. or B.S. Degree).
1. _____ 3. _____
2. _____ 4. _____

Advanced College Study (Graduate Degree, M.A. or M.S.)
1. _____ 3. _____
2. _____ 4. _____

Special Experience (Occupations that require a combination of training and work experience)
1. _____ 3. _____
2. _____ 4. _____

Appendix 7-6

SCHOOL SUBJECTS AND CAREERS

In this activity, identify three occupations that may be related to the school subjects listed here.

English/Language Arts

1. _____
2. _____
3. _____

Mathematics

1. _____
2. _____
3. _____

Fine Arts (Art, Music, Drama)

1. _____
2. _____
3. _____

History/Government
Social Studies

1. _____
2. _____
3. _____

Science (Biology, Chemistry, Physics, etc.)

1. _____
2. _____
3. _____

Practical Arts (Home Ec, Industrial Arts, etc.)

1. _____
2. _____
3. _____

Appendix 7-7

CAREER SETTINGS

Under the thirteen clusters below, list three settings where people may work when they are employed in that field. Consider the *places* where people work, not the specific jobs which they perform.

Example: *Health and Medicine:*

1. Hospital
2. Medical laboratory
3. Public health center

Communication and Media

1. _____
2. _____
3. _____

Sales and Distribution

1. _____
2. _____
3. _____

Engineering and Technology

1. _____
2. _____
3. _____

Public Service

1. _____
2. _____
3. _____

Personal Service
1. _____
2. _____
3. _____

Environment
1. _____
2. _____
3. _____

Transportation
1. _____
2. _____
3. _____

Building and Construction
1. _____
2. _____
3. _____

Manufacturing and Industry
1. _____
2. _____

Social Service
1. _____
2. _____
3. _____

Business, Computer
1. _____
2. _____
3. _____

Hospitality and Recreation
1. _____
2. _____
3. _____

Fine Arts and Entertainment
1. _____
2. _____
3. _____

Other
1. _____
2. _____

Appendix 7-8

AN APPRAISAL OF MY INTERESTS

CLUBS AND ORGANIZATIONS
(Include length of membership, record of participation, and offices held)

Organization	Things I Dislike	Things I Like

SOCIAL LIFE

Activity	Things I Dislike	Things I Like

HOBBIES, MAGAZINES, ETC.

Activity	Things I Dislike	Things I Like

Appendix 7-9

AN APPRAISAL OF MY APTITUDE

Aptitude means your capacity for success in a given area provided you receive information or training. Listed below are several areas of aptitude. On the right are three degrees of aptitude. Consider each item and check the degree to which you currently possess aptitude in that area. BA = Below Average, A = Average, AA = Above Average

```
                              DEGREE OF APTITUDE
                              BA       A       AA
```

1. Physical strength, coordination _____
2. Hand and finger dexterity _____
3. Mechanical _____
4. Clerical speed and accuracy _____
5. Leadership _____
6. Ability to get along with others _____
7. Musical _____
8. Artistic _____
9. Intellectual, understand ideas expressed in words _____
10. Visualize objects in three dimensions _____
11. Solve problems using logic _____
12. Work with numbers accurately _____
13. Write and talk easily _____
14. Recall past experiences _____

Appendix 7-10

AN APPRAISAL OF MY ABILITIES

Indicate: BA = Below Average, A = Average, AA = Above average

SUBJECTS	GRADES	I DISLIKE	I LIKE
English _____			
Math _____			

Science _____
_____
_____

Social Studies _____
_____
_____

Other _____
_____
_____

Appendix 7-11

MY AUTOBIOGRAPHY

A. FAMILY
Name _____ Date of Birth _____
Address _____
Father's Name _____ Career _____
Setting _____ Advantages _____
Mother's Name _____ Career _____
Setting _____ Advantages _____
Career(s) of Older Brother(s) _____
Career(s) of Older Sister(s) _____

B. Describe the things in your past or present which will make your autobiography a complete history of you. Include experiences or influences which have affected your personality, interests, or problems. Include the careers you considered, but decided against.

C. Write about past and current part-time jobs, possible future part-time jobs, educational plans and long-term career goals. Discuss briefly the careers you would like to learn about.

Appendix 7-12

EVALUATION FORM

1. Three current careers that are of interest to me are:
   1. _____
   2. _____
   3. _____
2. The first career I listed appeals to me because:
_____
_____

Cont'd

3. The second career I listed appeals to me because:
   _____
   _____

4. The third career I listed appeals to me because:
   _____
   _____

5. To prepare for the first career I would:
   _____
   _____

6. To prepare for the second career I would:
   _____
   _____

7. To prepare for the third career I would:
   _____
   _____

8. The reasons I would be well prepared and competitive in these careers are:
   _____
   _____
   _____

REFERENCES

Herbert, Deborah (Ed.): Career guidance, families and school counselors. Highlights, An ERIC/CAPS Digest in *The School Counselor* June 1987.

Kelly, Joan M. & Volz-Patton, Ruth: *Career Skills.* Encino, Glencoe, 1987.

Kelly, Joan M. & Volz-Patton, Ruth: *Student Activity Workbook: Career Skills.* Encino, Glencoe, 1987.

McHolland, James D.: Values auction. *Leader's Manual of the Human Potential Seminars* (Rev. 1975).

Chapter Eight

DEVELOP INDIVIDUAL POTENTIAL

INDIVIDUAL STUDENT GROWTH THROUGH GROUP COUNSELING

BARBARA MCCANN

Introduction

Group counseling in a high school fills many needs. It fulfills the adolescent need to belong to a group, to express feelings confidentially in a safe environment, to be heard by others who care, and to practice positive communication and problem solving skills.

Some experienced leaders of group counseling prefer to lead growth groups in which members work on different concerns. They believe that growth is achieved by being in a heterogeneous group and that everyone can benefit from involvement in a growth group.

Leadership of Growth Groups

Growth groups are unstructured; there is no specific plan for each session. Instead, members work on individual goals, and the leader selects activities that he/she ascertains would result in members learning specific skills at particular times. Only experienced group leaders should lead growth groups and these leaders must know when to intervene in the group to make it a worthwhile group experience, not just a rap or complaint session. School time is limited and valuable, and if the members are not learning from the group, it should be concluded. Counselors who are implementing a new group counseling program are advised to first lead structured groups, or co-lead their first growth groups with an experienced co-leader.

Goals

The goals for the growth group are to provide each member with the experience of:

- Being heard, understood and accepted in a non-judgmental way.
- Listening to other members of the group in a non-judgmental way.
- Thinking about and expressing personal feelings in a confidential, non-threatening setting.
- Receiving honest feedback from peers.
- Setting an individual goal and identifying the means to achieve it.

Individual goals within the growth group vary. They may include but are not limited to: improving a self-image, being accepted by others, sharing feelings, reducing stress, understanding others better, solving problems, and developing coping skills. The counselor may also introduce issues such as substance abuse, prejudice, school achievement, eating disorders, depression, and single-parent or blended families.

Publicizing the Group

Participation in the growth group must be voluntary. However, the counselor may need to describe this group to the students so they are aware of the opportunity and responsibility of being a member of the growth group. The counselor can be creative in demonstrating or defining the growth group. Some suggestions include: (1) leading students in a mini-group experience, (2) publicizing in school publications, and (3) suggesting group participation to eligible students.

Mini-Group Session:

Meeting with ninth grade students in small groups for one session during the first quarter offers an opportunity to involve students in a mini-group experience. The counselor presents several subjects to which the members may respond by going around the circle, each providing his/her own answers. Any member may pass if the question is uncomfortable for him/her. The questions may start with (1) What is your name? (2) Where did you go to school last year? (3) What do you like most about this school? (4) What do you like least about this school? (5) What do you miss most from your old school? (6) What were your greatest fears about coming to this school?

After this mini-group meeting, the counselor explains that this experience is similar to a growth group, where individual feelings are expressed and listened to by group members. The counselor gives the students information about group counseling "Questions and Answers," (Appendix 2-2), "I Would Like To Talk About...." (Appendix 8-1), and "Interested in a Growth Group?" (Appendix 8-2).

Publicizing in School Publications:

In addition to publicizing in school publications, previous members of growth groups frequently bring eligible members to discuss group membership with the counselor. The counselor gives them the description of the growth group and the questionnaires.

Personal Contact with the Counselor: The counselor is aware that certain students would benefit from the growth group experience, although these students may be hesitant to express an interest. Students who are shy, socially inept, culturally different, new to the school, not accepted into a peer group, undergoing family difficulties, stressed about grades or poor school achievements, or overly scheduled in many activities may hesitate to seek information. If the counselor meets with such students, explains the growth group, suggests that these students would learn from this experience, or encourages the students to come to talk about what they would like to get out of a group, the students may express an interest and gain from participating.

Group Selection

Meeting individually with prospective members provides opportunity for the counselor to have some perception as to whether the applicant would benefit from this particular group, would listen to others, and would help others learn, as well as learn from others. After meeting with all who are interested, the counselor selects members for a heterogeneous group, providing a balance of concerns. The counselor attempts to avoid the neighborhood effect, having best friends, neighbors, or a dating couple in the same group.

Definition of the Group

The growth group is a heterogeneous, multi-cultural group including males and females of different academic levels, popular and unpopular students. Members benefit from getting to know peers who are different from themselves; they gain understanding and respect for those whom they usually would not know, and would not associate with nor choose as friends. As members grow to appreciate members who are different from themselves, they also grow to be less suspicious and fearful of others who are different.

Sessions

Each session starts with answering the question, "How are you feeling today?" There is also an invitation, "Does anyone have anything they would like to talk about today?" "Does anyone have anything they would like to tell another member or ask another member?" In this respect the group sessions are open-ended or unstructured.

The first session begins with a review of the purpose and definition of the growth group. "Suggestions to Facilitate Communication" (Appendix 8-3) are distributed and discussed. These rules are used as guidelines in every session and are reviewed with the members intermittently.

During the first session members may practice formulating "I Messages" (When ... I felt ... because ...) (Gordon, 1975). They may practice their "I Messages" in dyads, then repeat them for the entire group. The members may explain to whom, when, and how they would like to use the "I Message," and practice using the "I Message" in the group until they feel comfortable and the group is assured that they can state their feelings convincingly to the person outside the group.

Topics

Topics in growth groups have included relating to peers, being picked on, getting along with siblings, boyfriends, girlfriends; relating to adults, parents, step-parents, teachers, bosses; improving academic problems, concern about homework and/or grades, and working through problems such as how to deal with pressure, guilt, depression, suicide, and death.

The leader may begin a session with open-ended topics such as "What is the best and/or worst thing that happened to you this week?" "What is something you are looking forward to, or something you dread?" "What is one thing you are proud of or one thing you fear?"

Activities conducted during sessions may involve setting priorities, putting lists in rank order, practicing "I Messages," listening actively, helping members define personal dependence and independence on a continuum, explaining privacy circles, constructing personal shields, or sharing feelings toward authority figures. The leader designs activities to meet the needs of the group members.

The leader invites feedback from members of the group, and may use the empty chair activity, success bombardment, "I like myself because...," or "I particularly like it when you...." Individual sessions or all sessions may be summarized or evaluated with the "I Learned Statements" (Appendix 7-3).

The leader of growth groups must be astute to identify the needs of the members at any given time and then be flexible and resourceful to provide meaningful follow-up activities to provide insight and skills. This leader must know when to allow the group to flow without structure, when to intervene, and when to add structure to the group activity so that each session is meaningful.

Evaluation

The author has led growth groups every semester for approximately sixteen years. During the last session of the growth group experience, members complete anonymously the "Group Counseling Evaluation" (Appendix 8-4). Answers that some members have written to questions 7, 8, 9, and 10 (Appendix 8-4) are given below.

7. The thing I liked best about the group was:

... "being able to talk about problems and listen to what people in similar situations would do."

... "the openness of everybody."

... "getting to know other people and knowing that we all basically share the same problems."

... "I realized other people's problems and it helped me relate to my own."

... "I could talk and not feel left out."

... "We could talk about ourselves without being afraid that the whole world will know."

8. The thing I liked least about the group was:

... "It was too short—sometimes missed class."

... "missing work in class."

... "the first day."

... "the large size, smaller groups are better."
... "the short period of time we had to meet."

9. What I learned most from the group was:

   ... "Everyone has problems and it's easier to talk about them with others."
   ... "you can't put people into stereo-types and judge them at fair value."
   ... "feelings."
   ... "communication."
   ... "self-respect."
   ... "that other people have problems other than me and that I'm not as bad off as I think."
   ... "to listen."

10. If people were to ask me about the group, I would say:

    ... "It is a good experience and a good way to meet people."
    ... "It will help you a lot if you have problems."
    ... "It was fun."
    ... "I liked it."
    ... "Give it a shot."

Appendix 8-1

I WOULD LIKE TO TALK ABOUT....

_____ my grades _____ my weight _____ dating
_____ my study habits _____ my health _____ my fears
_____ being shy _____ making friends _____ being bored
_____ my boyfriend _____ my girlfriend
_____ getting along with my teachers
_____ getting along with my friends
_____ getting along with my parents
_____ getting along with my brothers/sisters
_____ death of someone close to me
_____ what I am going to do after high school
_____ moving to a new school
_____ problems with drinking of someone I know
_____ problems with drugs of someone I know
_____ other problems someone I know has
_____ my parents' divorce or remarriage
_____ getting into trouble _____ something else

- -

I would like to be in group counseling.
Date _____ Signature _____

Appendix 8-2

INTERESTED IN A GROWTH GROUP?

Name _____ Grade _____ Date _____

Directions: Answer the following questions with "YES" or "NO."
1. _____ I would like to be in group counseling right away.
   _____ Although I am interested in being in a group I have no pressing needs right now and it is O.K. if I do it later on in the year.
2. I would describe myself as shy _____, quiet _____, talkative _____, outgoing _____.
   I can be a good listener. _____
   I can keep things confidential. _____
3. I would be willing to meet after school. _____
   _____ Tuesdays (2:45–3:30)
   _____ Wednesdays (2:45–3:30)
   _____ Thursdays (2:45–3:30)

Appendix 8-3

SUGGESTIONS TO FACILITATE COMMUNICATION

In addition to the ground rules, Appendix 1-6, these suggestions help facilitate communication in groups.

1. Look directly at the person being spoken to, or the person speaking to you.
2. Speak directly *to* a member, not to the leader or another member *about* a member.
3. Listen attentively. Allow each person to finish his/her statement. Do not interrupt.
4. Pay attention to the speaker. Only one person may speak at a time.
5. Speak only for yourself. Use first person. Say "I" did or thought, or felt, not "you." You can only speak for yourself, not others.
6. Avoid being judgmental. Do not use "put-down" or "killer" statements. Try to phrase things positively. Be sincere, not sarcastic.
7. Say "I won't," not "I can't." It is usually more accurate.
8. Show attention, do not do distracting things, lean forward and maintain eye contact. Show you care about others.
9. Learn and use the "I Message" when appropriate. "I feel _____ when _____ because _____."
10. Listen beyond others' words, for their feelings. "You may be feeling _____ because _____. Is this how you feel?" Then *listen* as the other person explains his/her feelings.

Appendix 8-4

GROWTH GROUP EVALUATION

Directions: Indicate your answers to the first six items by drawing a circle around Yes or No. Complete the open-ended statements for items seven through ten. If you would like to be in another group please write this on the separate piece of paper, giving your name so the counselor can contact you. Thank you.

1. The growth group experience improved my understanding of others.
   Yes No
2. The growth group had no effect on me. Yes No
3. The growth group had some effect on my behavior outside the group.
   Yes No
4. I disliked being a member of this growth group. Yes No
5. The group improved my understanding of myself. Yes No
6. I would recommend a similar growth group experience for my friends.
   Yes No

7. The thing I liked best about this growth group was _____

8. The thing I liked least about this growth group was _____

9. I learned most from the group _____

10. If people were to ask me about my experience in this growth group I would say _____

REFERENCE

Gordon, Thomas: Putting "I–Messages" to work. *Parent Effectiveness Training.* N.Y., Wyden, 1975.

Chapter Nine

DEVELOP POSITIVE HUMAN RELATIONS AMONG ETHNIC GROUPS

GETTING TO KNOW YOU: RACE RELATIONS IS EVERYBODYS' RESPONSIBILITY

GEORGIA G. RIDDICK

Rationale

Educators need to be sensitive to the ethnic tension and conflict within their schools. Counselors may be the first in the school to learn of racial tension or acts that cause students to feel they are the focus of hostility.

The author, who has been a teacher/counselor in three different multi-ethnic high schools, has observed incidents which point out the need for students to understand and respect each other, and each other's cultural heritage:

- Some students isolate themselves from students of different origins in classrooms or the cafeteria.
- Some students keep a low profile and do not volunteer to answer questions in class, although they know the answers, because they do not want to attract attention to themselves.
- Some students treat students in other ethnic groups as though they are non-persons. These students direct all of their comments to the students within their own group even when others are present.
- Some students belittle or use disparaging comments when referring to students in other ethnic groups such as "those foreigners," "those blacks," "those whites," "those dumb cheaters," "those lazy bums," or "those no-goods."
- Some students refuse to let students of other ethnic groups pass in the hallways until, in praying-hands fashion, they beg to be allowed to pass.

- Some students of one ethnic group are bombarded with eggs in the school cafeteria.
- Some students express fear for their physical safety.
    a. One group of students is chased by another group of students.
    b. Some students panic when they are given schedule changes because they say they have been threatened by some students who are in the new class.
    c. Some students enlist other students as "bodyguards."
    d. Some students state that they believe they must carry weapons to protect themselves.

Fish (1970) reported that most of the conflict in high schools in the United States was related to problems of race. Furthermore, he stated that individuals who fostered conflict typically harbored feelings of suspicion, distrust, and fear and sometimes these feelings were mixed with hatred for people of other races (Fish, 1970).

Tsui and Sammons (1988) report that racial discrimination is common among young Vietnamese who have distinctive American features that have made them targets of discrimination in their own country and their own culture in this country.

Education is adversely affected when there is a breakdown in human relations in a school. Conflicts must be recognized, acknowledged, and addressed. Counselors must act *before* learning gives way to protest activities or to fighting.

People fight when they feel threatened and fearful of other people or behavior that they do not understand. Krumboltz and Krumboltz (1972) describe the "Fear Reduction Principle" as a method for helping people overcome their fears of particular situations. Exposure to the feared situations gradually is increased while the fearful person is otherwise comfortable, relaxed, and secure. This basic principle can be applied when young people fear persons of different cultures and/or races. Attitudes of fearful and bigoted high school students can be changed as these young people are exposed to students of different cultures and/or races that they do not understand, while the fearful students are in an atmosphere of trust, acceptance, respect, warmth, open communication, and understanding.

Authorities (Dinkmeyer and Muro, 1971; Berkovitz, 1975) agree that group counseling in the high school setting has many particular advantages to bringing about change in attitudes and behaviors.

Fish (1970) and Berkovitz (1975) confirm that group counseling programs can prevent explosive growth of ethnic tension and conflict within schools. As group members get to know each other and discover areas they have in common, such as problems in their individual lives, they become more open, and express their feelings about those different from themselves (Berkovitz, 1975). Fish (1970) supports the effectiveness of counseling groups as a method to bring about changes in attitudes. He states:

- Direct participation in a group in which one can recount personal experiences is more effective in reducing prejudice than instruction or discussion about cultural facts and contributions.
- Group experiences featuring individual attention, role-playing, and psychodramas are effective in inducing change in attitudes, especially if the participants continue to experience reinforcement and support of the group.
- Knowledge that individuals of another race share some of one's own values and beliefs increases a person's acceptance of people of other races.

Tsui and Sammons (1988) also affirm that group counseling is the best means to provide counseling to adolescent Vietnamese refugees. They add that the preventive model that is educational, supportive, and of a problem-solving nature, is more acceptable to Southeast Asians than individual or insight-oriented counseling.

Definition of the Group

Members are screened individually (Appendix 1-5). The leader selects eight to ten students from the tenth and eleventh grades who volunteer to try to improve human relations among students in their high school. Male and female students representing the ethnic make-up of the school are selected. Students should have adequate English speaking skills to express themselves. The leader selects two or three role models from different races who acknowledge that they were prejudiced or were victims of prejudice, but currently are accepting of students different from themselves. These role models are accepted by all ethnic groups in the school.

This group meets for eleven sessions, one hour per week, and the time is rotated so members miss each class every sixth week. Activities for this group are selected from references that the counselors may want to have available: Canfield, 1976; Fromkin and Sherwood, 1976; Johnson, 1972; Pfeiffer and Jones Handbooks 1973–1989; Trotzer, 1989.

Publicity

Flyers (Appendix 9-1) are distributed to tenth and eleventh grade students in English classes, English as a Second Language (ESL) classes, the cafeteria, and the guidance office. The group is described in the school's daily bulletin and on the public address system.

Goals

At the end of this group experience, members will be able to:
- Initiate getting acquainted with students of different races.
- Show evidence of active listening when communicating with a person of a different race.
- Recognize personal experiences, feelings and values that they have in common with students of different races and/or cultures.
- Recognize and begin to question their fears and prejudices of people different from themselves.
- Recognize the variety of ways in which they are perceived by their peers.
- Share feelings and ideas with students of different races.

Ground Rules

In addition to the ground rules (Appendix 1-6), this group should be aware of and review the "Suggestions to Facilitate Communication" (Appendix 8-3).

Sessions

Session 1

Purpose: The members will be able to:
- Get acquainted with the leader and with each other.
- Learn and practice the ground rules.

Develop Positive Human Relations Among Ethnic Groups 127

- Participate in the get-acquainted activity.
- Begin individual goal setting.

Procedure of the Leader:

1. Introduce yourself and the members to each other.
2. Present the ground rules for the group.
3. Explain the directions for "Getting to Know You" (Appendix 9-2), and assign the first dyad partners.
4. Distribute copies of the questions for the "Getting to Know You" activity (Appendix 9-3).
5. Conduct the activity, calling time at three minute intervals, when members are to find new dyad partners.
6. Lead a discussion with the entire group based on questions:
   a. What did you learn from this activity?
   b. Did you discover that you share anything in common with any other group members?
   c. What feelings did you experience as you participated in this activity?
7. Discuss the "Guidelines for Goal Setting." In addition to the criteria listed in Appendix 1-7, goals for this group should be related to understanding and getting along with others.
8. Give members cards and ask them to think of one personal goal to accomplish during this group. Ask members to write their goals on the cards.
9. Summarize this session.

Session 2

Purpose: The members will be able to:

- Clarify goals.
- Get better acquainted through self-disclosure.

Procedure of the Leader:

1. Re-emphasize the importance of confidentiality.
2. Ask members to choose one question from Appendix 9-3 and discuss their answers with the group.
3. Ask volunteers to tell how it felt to discuss their answers with the group.
4. Explain the "Goal-Structuring Exercise."

a. Review the guidelines for goal setting from last session.
b. Post and discuss the "Goal Setting Criteria" (Appendix 1-7).
c. Share your own goal and explain how it meets the criteria, using it as an example to answering the questions (Appendix 1-7).
d. Assign members to dyads.
e. Ask each dyad partner in turn, to read the goal that he/she wrote in the previous session. The partners clarify each goal, using the questions.
f. Suggest that each partner revise his/her goal to make it specific and realistic.
g. Ask partners to discuss barriers that may impede them from reaching their goals and then list ways that they can overcome these barriers.
5. Assemble the entire group.
6. Ask members to share with the group their reactions to the "Goal-Structuring" activity and the reasons they would like to achieve their specific goals.
7. Give members copies of the "I Learned Statements" (Appendix 7-3) and ask them to complete as many items as applicable.

Session 3

Purpose: Members will be able to:

- Experience a climate of trust in the group.
- Give and receive positive feedback.

Procedure of the Leader:

1. Instruct members to complete the "About Me" questionnaire (Appendix 9-4). Ask members to put their social security numbers or phone numbers on their answer sheets so they can compare their answers now with their answers at the termination of the group.
2. Ask members if they want to discuss any particular items.
3. Remind members to work on their individual goal.
4. Begin the "Positive Feelings" activity by saying one thing that you recall that a member did last week that helped another member

feel positive about him/her-self. Encourage members to recall positive things about each other.
5. Ask members to describe how they felt when giving and receiving positive feedback. They may use the feeling vocabulary (Appendix 5-2).
6. Ask volunteers to summarize their perceptions of what was accomplished during this group session.

Session 4

Purpose: Members will be able to:
- Recognize that accepting themselves is a pre-requisite to accepting others.

Procedure of the Leader:
1. Re-emphasize confidentiality.
2. Remind members to work on their individual goals.
3. Lead a "Strength-Bombardment" exercise, Chapter twelve, Session 4.
4. Process the exercise by having members share their reactions, and answer the following questions:
    a. When other group members added to your list of strengths how did you feel?
    b. How do you perceive yourself to be regarded by other group members?
    c. Do you feel differently about yourself after doing the activity than you did prior to the activity? Describe.
5. Link commonalities of members whenever possible.
6. Summarize the session.
7. Give members cards on which they write words to describe their impressions of this session (Appendix 2-3). They may also include suggestions for improvement. Responses are anonymous and members drop their cards in a box as they leave the session.
8. Tell members that next week they will be asked about their progress on their personal goals.

Session 5

Purpose: Members will be able to:
- Actively listen to other members.
- Express positive attributes of others.
- Review the progress they have made toward achieving their goals.

Procedure of the Leader:
1. Ask a volunteer to review the previous session.
2. Review the group goals and ask members to discuss their perceptions of these goals.
3. Ask members to evaluate their progress toward achieving these group goals.
4. Ask members to remember their individual goals. Give members magic markers and large sheets of paper and give the following directions:
   a. Fold the sheet in half once and then in half again so it is divided into four equal sections.
   b. In the upper left quarter draw a picture or symbol or write a word to indicate your progress toward accomplishing your individual goal.
   c. In the lower left quarter of the sheet, draw a picture, symbol or word to describe the barriers to achieving that goal.
   d. In the upper right quarter list the things that you can do to overcome or remove the barriers.
   e. In the lower right quarter, draw pictures, symbols or words to indicate:
   (1) your feelings at this moment.
   (2) your feelings after your goal has been achieved.
5. Ask members to share their completed sheets with the group.
6. Ask members to share how they recognize acceptance from other people. Lead a discussion on communicating acceptance and members may role play how they show acceptance or how others show disdain. "Communicating Acceptance To Other Individuals" may be used as an activity (Johnson, 1972).
7. Assign homework: "Give one person a well-deserved compliment before the next session."
8. Give members cards to write their impressions of this session.

Session 6

Purpose: Members will be able to:

- Trust other group members enough to discuss their feelings.
- Resolve interpersonal conflicts through role-reversal.

Procedure of the Leader:

1. Review the giving and receiving of acceptance and compliments.
2. Distribute felt-tip pens and sheets of paper.
3. Conduct the activity, "A Here-And-Now-Face," adapted from Kranzow, 1973, in Trotzer, 1989.
    a. Draw a face that represents the feelings you have right now.
    b. Below the face, write a verbal description of these feelings, and possible reasons.
    c. Share drawings with the group, describing feelings. Include both what the feelings are and the reasons they exist.
4. Lead the activity, "Role Reversal Exercise" (Appendix 9-5).
5. Ask a volunteer to summarize the important points learned during this session.

Session 7

Purpose: Members will be able to:

- Develop trust by experiencing appropriate risk-taking.

Procedure of the Leader:

1. Reduce tension among members by giving them the option to pass from an activity.
2. Provide directions for the activity, "Trust Walk" (Trotzer, 1989).
3. Lead a discussion of the experience in relation to: trusting oneself, trusting others, and being a trustworthy friend.
4. Explain the activity "Receiving Feedback Through Metaphors." Describe and give examples of metaphors. Members volunteer, one at a time, to receive metaphors as feedback from other members. Going around the circle, other members use metaphors to describe their positive impressions of the member designated as the receiver. The volunteer receiver must be silent throughout the time that this feedback is given.

5. Continue the activity until all members who desire feedback have volunteered to be the "silent" member.
6. Ask for overall reactions of members concerning this activity.
7. Summarize this session, linking commonalities wherever possible.

Session 8

Purpose: The members will be able to:

- Examine their own emotional reactions to the physical characteristics of others.
- Learn to observe others, noting positive as well as negative aspects of people different from themselves.
- Learn the effects of generalizing and stereotyping people.

Procedure of the Leader:

1. Distribute copies of "A Partial List of Prejudices" (Appendix 9-6).
2. Ask members to identify the items that describe physical characteristics of people.
3. Ask them to rank their initial reactions to items as positive (+), neutral (0), or negative (−). Note the negatives.
4. Have members discuss their initial reactions in dyads.
5. Ask them to discuss their initial reactions in the entire group.
6. Give adjectives (Appendix 2-3) to the members and ask them to give their impressions of this session.

Session 9

Purpose: The members will be able to:

- Share feelings and ideas about prejudices in a non-threatening manner.
- Explore the validity of common prejudices.

Procedure of the Leader:

1. Prepare ten cards before this session, each card with one prejudice listed. Choose from items listed in Appendix 9-6 or write appropriate prejudices for this group.
2. Give each member a blank card and a pencil.
3. Read the list of ten prejudices from the prepared cards. Ask

participants to write one additional object of prejudice on their blank card.
4. Collect cards and add them to the ten prepared cards.
5. Divide members into triads. Give directions.
    a. One member from each triad takes two cards off the top of the stack, looks at both cards and selects one. The other card is returned to the stack. These members return to their triad, facing the other two members of the triad.
    b. The member of the triad with the card announces the topic of his/her card to the other two members. These members verbally assault, make disparaging or stereotyped remarks about the subject of prejudice, while the member holding the card refutes their statements and defends the person or group being attacked.
    c. Call time after three minutes.
    d. Other triad members take turns at being the person to select a card and defend the object of prejudice.
6. Lead the total group in a discussion of the following:
    a. What types of prejudicial statements were made by the participants?
    b. How did members feel when they perceived themselves as the stereo-typed object of prejudice?
    c. Which comments were the most hurtful?
    d. How may such comments affect the self-esteem of these persons?
    e. How did the defending members defend the objects of prejudice?
    f. How did members feel when they were making stereotypical remarks?
    g. What did members learn about their own prejudices, perceptions, and behaviors?
7. Lead a discussion of the fallacies of typical prejudice in society, the results of such attitudes, and ways to deal with or refute them.
8. Ask a volunteer to summarize the session.

Session 10

Purpose: The members will be able to:
- Assess the extent to which they achieved their personal goals.

- Evaluate the changes in attitude members have made with respect to stereotyping and prejudice.
- Discuss closure of the group.

Procedure of the Leader:

1. Review the activity conducted last week and ask if any members thought about the experience during the week. Discuss.
2. Instruct members to complete the "About Me" questionnaire again (Appendix 9-4).
3. Give members their previous answers and ask them to compare their answers and mark differences in the left margin next to the item numbers. Ask their permission to keep a record of the differences, with their names.
4. Ask members to share the extent to which they achieved their individual goals.
5. Give directions and conduct the activity: "Hope Chest" Chapter one, Proposal one.
6. Re-emphasize the agreement to maintain confidentiality, and stress that confidentiality continues even after the group has terminated.
7. Share personal feelings about ending this group.
8. Offer to meet with members individually and inform them about the reunion of the group three weeks from this session.

Session 11

(Three Weeks Later)

Purpose: The members will be able to:
- State the extent to which they continue to meet the goals of the group and their individual goals.
- Brainstorm suggestions as to how to continue to improve human relations in the school.

Procedure of the Leader:

1. Greet members.
2. Ask volunteers to talk about the progress they made on the group goals and their individual goals.
3. Ask members to complete the final evaluations (Appendix 9-7).

4. Ask members for recommendations to continue to improve understanding and good human relations in this school.

Appendix 9-1

GETTING TO KNOW YOU

A Counseling Group for Any Student Who:

1. Wants to be better understood by other people.
2. Would like to talk with students who have similar interests and concerns.
3. Would like to talk with students who have different interests and concerns.
4. Is willing to listen to other students talk about their concerns.
5. Would like to help students in our school get acquainted, understand, and respect each other.

Interested students contact Mr./Mrs. _____ in the Counseling Office.

Appendix 9-2

GETTING TO KNOW YOU

Adapted from Gillies, 1973
Excerpt from *My Needs, Your Needs, Our Needs*
by Jerry Gillies, 1974,
Used by permission of Doubleday, a division of Bantam,
Doubleday, Dell Publishing Group, Inc.

Directions: You will be assigned your first dyad partner and then you will have different partners every three minutes. You will be given copies of questions and during each three minute interval you are to discuss and listen to your partner discuss answers to three questions.
1. Answer the first three questions with your first dyad partner, each partner in turn. You will be given three minutes for both of you to answer these three questions.
2. At the end of three minutes the leader will call time, and you are to find new partners. Both partners in the second dyads will answer questions numbered four through six within the next three minutes.
3. Continue to change partners every three minutes until you have shared information about yourselves with all other group members. (Approximately thirty minutes).

Appendix 9-3

QUESTIONS FOR THE "GETTING TO KNOW YOU" ACTIVITY

1. How would your mother or father describe you as a child age six to ten?
2. What was your favorite toy as a child?
3. What is your favorite toy now?
- -
4. What were you most proud of as a child?
5. What was your childhood nickname and how did you feel about it?
6. Do you like your first name now? If not, what would you like instead?
- -
7. What is your favorite possession?
8. Name a favorite possession you no longer possess, and describe your feelings about no longer having it.
9. What is the funniest thing that ever happened to you?
- -
10. What is the silliest thing you have ever done?
11. What is the stupidest thing you have ever done?
12. What is your all-time favorite movie? Why does it have special meaning for you?
- -
13. What is your favorite book? What is there about the book that has personal meaning for you?
14. With what fictional hero or heroine do you most closely identify?
15. How good a friend are you? Give an example.
- -
16. With which member of your family do you most identify? Why?
17. If you had to be someone else instead of yourself, whom would you choose?
18. Who is your best friend of the same sex? What do you like about this person?
- -
19. Who is your best friend of the opposite sex? What do you like about this person?
20. What do you look for most in a friend?
21. Name something you hate to do. What do you hate about it?
- -
22. What in life is most important to you?
23. What do you like most about this group?
24. What do you like least about this group?
- -

Appendix 9-4

THE "ABOUT ME" QUESTIONNAIRE

Directions: Answer the following questions by putting the first letter in the blank designating:

Frequently   Seldom   Never

1. I have things in common with group members who are different from me.
2. Being in a counseling group is a worthwhile experience. _____
3. I find it easy to talk to people of different races. _____
4. I am interested in what others have to say. _____
5. I am sarcastic to people. _____
6. I try to support and encourage other people even if they are different from me. _____
7. I don't like people butting in when I am with my friends. _____
8. When I am with a group that criticizes others it does not bother me as long as those that are criticized are not my friends. _____
9. I make fun of people who are different from me. _____
10. I try to find out what kind of reactions my behavior produces on other people. _____
11. I feel at ease with group members who are different from me. _____
12. I feel free to talk about my personal experiences with people who are different from me. _____
13. I believe that people who come from other countries will never be *real* Americans. _____
14. I believe that the more a person is different from me, the less he/she can be trusted. _____
15. I like to meet students that I do not know. _____
16. I believe that other students see me differently from the way I see myself. _____
17. I feel accepted by other group members. _____
18. I feel comfortable at this school. _____
19. I would rather be in class than in the halls or at lunch because I am uncomfortable if there is no adult around. _____
20. I find it easier to write about my experiences than to talk with other members about them. _____
21. The more different a person is from me, the more uncomfortable I feel with him/her. _____
22. I can trust other members of this group. _____
23. I can trust other students in this school. _____
24. This group has a warm atmosphere that makes it easy to talk about myself. _____

cont'd

25. I show my dislike to some-one because he/she is different from me and my friends. _____
26. I feel more comfortable in this group than I do in the school in general. _____
27. I recommend this counseling group to my friends. _____
28. I believe that the group leader cares about me and is interested in what I say. _____

Appendix 9-5

A ROLE REVERSAL EXERCISE

Purpose:
- Gain insight into how the other person perceives the conflict situation.
- Increase the level of acceptance and understanding that members have for each other.

Procedure:
1. Pick a current topic of interest on which there are differences of opinion in the group. Example: Should metal detectors and drug-detecting dogs be allowed in schools?
2. Divide the group in half, with each subgroup representing one side of the issue.
3. Instruct each subgroup to meet separately for fifteen minutes to prepare their side of the issue in negotiations with members of the other subgroup.
4. Pair each person in one subgroup with a person in the opposite subgroup; each pair thus consists of persons representing opposite sides of the issue.
5. In the pair, one person is designated A and the other person is designated B. Person A is given three minutes to present his/her side of the issue. Person B then reverses his/her role by presenting to Person A the position as if he were Person A.
6. Person B then is given three minutes to present his/her side of the issue. Person A then reverses his/her role by presenting person B's position as if he/she were Person B.
7. Give the pairs five minutes to arrive at a joint agreement on the issue. During this five minutes they must obey the following rule: Before either can reply to a statement made by the other each must accurately and warmly paraphrase the other's statement to the other's satisfaction.
8. Lead the entire group in a discussion of the impact of role reversal upon their being able to understand and appreciate the other side of an issue:
    a. Did role reversal help you to reach an agreement?
    b. Did role reversal affect how you felt about each other during negotiations?
    c. How did you feel when you put yourself into the other person's place?
    d. How did you feel when the other person put him/her-self in your place?

Appendix 9-6

A PARTIAL LIST OF PREJUDICES

1. A person who wears funny clothes.
2. A man with hair below his shoulders.
3. An old woman with a lot of makeup on.
4. A person who is blind or visually impaired.
5. A person who is deaf or hearing impaired.
6. A person who laughs very loud.
7. A person who yells instead of talks.
8. A person who uses crutches.
9. A person who won't look at you when you talk.
10. A person who can't date, even though he/she is sixteen years old.
11. A person who dresses punk.
12. A person who criticizes other people.
13. A person who is makes fun of other people.
14. A person who wears a turban.
15. A person in a wheel chair.
16. A person who wears a cap indoors.
17. A person who wears a veil over their head.
18. A person who is Black.
19. A person who is White.
20. A person who was born in Asia, Africa, Israel, Europe, Iran, Afghanistan, Iraq, China, Japan, Viet Nam, Korea, Laos, Mexico, El Salvador, Alaska, Egypt, India, Soviet Union, Arabia.

Appendix 9-7

FINAL EVALUATION

Directions: Indicate your behavior in the group by writing the first letter in the blank, designating: Frequently, Seldom or Never.

1. I initiated conversations with students of different races. _____
2. I actively listened to others. _____
3. I learned about other students' feelings in this group. _____
4. I shared ideas with students of races different from my own. _____
5. I have tried to provide open and honest feedback to other students in this group. _____

Complete the following sentences:

6. One fear or prejudice that I had when I entered this group was _____
_____
7. I learned that other members of the group perceived me as _____

8. One experience that I have had that is in common with a student of another race is _____

9. One value that I have that is the same as that of a student of another race is _____

10. I believe I am more or less prejudiced than I was when I entered this group. _____

11. A possible reason is _____

12. One thing that helped me appreciate other members of this group was _____

13. Something else I want to say about this group experience is _____

REFERENCES

Berkovitz, I.H.: *When Schools Care.* N.Y., Brunner/Mazel, 1975.
Canfield, J. & Wells, H. C.: *100 Ways to Enhance Self-concept in the Classroom.* Englewood Cliffs, N.J., Prentice-Hall, 1976.
Dinkmeyer, D. C. & Muro, J. J.: *Group Counseling: Theory and Practice.* Itasca, F. E. Peacock, 1971.
Fish, K. L.: *Conflict and Dissent in the Schools.* N.Y., Bruce, 1970.
Fromkin, H. L. & Sherwood, J. J.: *Intergroup and Minority Relations: An Experiential Handbook.* La Jolla, University Associates, 1976.
Gillies, Jerry: *My Needs, Your Needs, Our Needs.* N.Y., Doubleday, 1974.
Johnson, D. W.: *Reaching Out: Interpersonal Effectiveness and Self-actualization.* Englewood Cliffs, Prentice-Hall, 1972.
Kranzow, G. W.: *Peer Counseling Handbook.* ESEA Title III, Peer Counseling Project. Special Education District of Lake County, Gurnee, IL. March 1973.
Krumboltz, J. D. & Krumboltz, H. B.: *Changing Children's Behavior.* Englewood Cliffs, Prentice-Hall, 1972.
Pfeiffer, J. W. & Jones, J. E.: *A Handbook of Structured Experiences for Human Relations Training.* San Diego: University Associates, 1973-1989.
Trotzer, J. P.: *The Counselor and the Group: Integrating Theory, Training, and Practice* (2nd Ed.). Muncie, Accelerated Development, 1989.
Tsui, Alice & Sammons, Morgan. Group intervention with adolescent Vietnamese refugees. *Journal for Specialists in Group Work.* 13, 2, May 1988.

Chapter Ten

LEARN TO HELP OTHERS

PREPARING PEER COUNSELORS TO WORK WITH YOUNGER STUDENTS

Elyse Carmichael

Rationale

Tindall and Gray (1985) define a peer counselor as a person who assumes the role of a helping person with contemporaries. The term "peer" denotes a person who shares related values, experiences, and life-style and is approximately the same age. Myrick and Erney (1979), in their book *Youth Helping Youth*, state that peer counseling is the most important educational concept in several years. These young people are learning to be effective listeners, role models and group leaders. Learning is enhanced and education is more effective as students facilitate personal development of themselves and others.

Peer counselors benefit from the specialized human relations training and the opportunity to help others which contributes to their own personal growth and development (Frenza, 1985). Helping others is not easy but can be rewarding. Myrick and Erney (1978) state, "So many people today are struggling to get along in this fast-paced and rapidly changing world that the need for helping services has increased in all areas. . . ." (p. 2).

The peer counselors in this high school work with students in their own school, make visits to the feeder intermediate schools to reassure these students about life at the high school, and, when specifically requested by the elementary counselor, also work with children in an elementary school. These peer counselors work with groups as well as individuals. As Tindall and Gray (1985) affirm, the peer counselor can be a vital assistant to the professional counselor by extending counseling services to more students than could be served by the professional counselor alone.

Huey (1985) writes that sixth grade and eighth grade students are fearful about entering a large, impersonal school. More is needed than just talking about the schedules and the academic subjects. Only through groups that provide clarification, discussion, questions and answers, and other interactive techniques, can future intermediate school and high school students increase their understanding and acceptance, and lose their fear. He writes, "The use of peer counselors in a structured, systematic group orientation program facilitates the delivery of vital school-related information" (p. 7).

This group proposal is a plan to provide training for high school peer counselors to work with elementary school students in groups. The high school students suggest the subjects for the groups. The high school students in peer counseling, with the supervision and resources provided by the co-leaders of the peer counseling group, develop the plans and materials that the peer counselors use with the elementary children.

As the peer counselors work for a common purpose they share information, receive mutual support, and gain individual confidence. As D'Andrea and Salovey (1983) stated when they led "the Bridge," a group of college peer counselors, collective action leads to a clearer sense of self. These authors, in the book *Peer Counseling Skills and Perspectives* (1983), write that peer counseling provides greater social and interpersonal skills for growth in personal life, understanding of individual psychology, group processes, and ways of facilitating communication and interaction.

As they work on this project, these high school peer counselors learn about group process. They then can apply these skills in many settings.

Goals

Peer Counselors Will:
- Recapture their own thoughts, feelings, and concerns as sixth grade students, so they can relate to the elementary students through sharing their experiences.
- Relate information about the group counseling process to the peer counseling class.
- Identify and prioritize subjects with written goals to relate to sixth grade students.

- Select appropriate activities that are age appropriate for sixth grade students to meet their written goals.
- Rehearse in the peer counseling class, using the plans and materials.
- Plan logistics to get to and from the elementary school within the peer counseling period.

Definition of the Group

Frenza (1985) states that in most secondary school peer counseling programs self-selection is used, in which virtually everyone who applies to the program is accepted. This is *not* the case in this program.

The peer counseling applicants of Marshall High School are screened each spring for the following year's elective class. Prospective group members are juniors or seniors and are referred by teachers, fellow students or themselves. Applicants complete an application, submit six confidential teacher evaluations, and are interviewed by a committee of previous peer counselors as well as by the co-leaders of the peer counseling class. Delworth and Brown (1977) indicate that basic qualifications of peer counselors should emphasize: commitment to helping others and the ability to interact with a variety of people; willingness to accept standards of ethical conduct such as confidentiality of information; and willingness and ability to work within the philosophy and goals of the program. The screening interviews are conducted to ascertain if the potential members have these qualities.

This class of eighteen students meets daily, and students receive an academic grade and one elective credit. A school counselor and a teacher co-lead the class. The peer counselors, prior to planning this project, met for fourteen weeks, one semester. During the first semester they learned and practiced listening and responding skills, and how to use these skills as a helping person. During the second semester they met with the sixth grade students weekly for approximately six sessions. The high school students planned this project of providing group counseling to elementary children during the third quarter so it could be implemented during the fourth quarter of the school year.

Sessions

Sessions 1 and 2

Procedure of the Leader:

1. Provide an overview for implementing this project.
2. Divide the group into two sub-groups, each with one leader, so members have a maximum opportunity to participate.
3. Ask members to remember concerns, feelings, and experiences that they had as sixth grade students, and enter them in their journals.
4. Lead a discussion of these journal entries with members of the sub-group.
5. Link the common threads of experiences of group members.
6. Ask group members to list the common concerns of sixth grade students.
7. Bring sub-groups together and discuss these concerns of sixth grade students.
8. Arrange for the elementary counselor to speak to the peer counselors.

Sessions 3 and 4

Procedure of the Leader:

1. Discuss the group process and group counseling. What does a group leader do to assure that group members learn and practice appropriate behaviors as a result of being in the group?
2. Present selected material from Corey and Corey (1987) in handouts for discussion of information.
3. Ask members to relate the information to interactions in the peer counselors' group.
4. Direct members to list in their journals the stages of the peer counseling group.
5. Help members to evaluate the peer counseling group and their own progress in the group process.

Session 5

Procedure of the Leader:

1. List the resources provided in sessions one through five, and ask students to select activities to present to the children.
2. Prepare questions for the elementary counselor.

Session 6

Procedure of the Leader:

1. Ask members to listen to the speaker, the elementary school counselor, and ask appropriate questions. Use this person as a resource.
2. With permission of the peer counselors, share the goals and plans of the group with this speaker who acts as a consultant.
3. Help students to identify and prioritize the subjects they plan to address with the sixth grade students.
4. Help the students write goal statements for the sixth grade students to achieve as a result of the groups.
5. Recommend that students discuss and revise goal statements.

Sessions 7 and 8

Procedure of the Leader:

1. Provide examples of materials that are appropriate for children. (Canfield and Wells, 1976, *100 Ways to Enhance Self-Concept in the Classroom;* Simon, 1974, *Meeting Yourself Halfway;* and Ratliffe and Herman, 1982, *Self-Awareness.*
2. Help peer counselors select and write activities to meet the specified goals.
3. Help peer counselors write simple group proposals for six sessions.

One format that has been successful for several years is:

Day 1: Peer counselors perform skits depicting typical problems new intermediate students face. Afterward students meet in pre-selected groups (elementary teacher or counselor assign the students to small groups) to get acquainted.

Days 2-5: Peer counselors discuss with the small groups transitional issues. One icebreaker is teaching the sixth grade students to use combination locks.

Day 6: Peer counselors close the groups and plan and conduct a final social activity. Sometimes this has been an extended lunch together followed by games.

Session 9

Procedure of the Leader:

1. Encourage group members to role play with the materials they have prepared.
2. Recommend to members that they evaluate the plans and materials and make changes when appropriate.

Session 10

Procedure of the Leader:

1. Show group members how to write individual journal entries about their own learning, feelings, and growth while developing this program.
2. Ask those who wish, to share their entries with the group.
3. Suggest that they make further revisions if they believe new ideas will improve their plans.

Session 11

Procedure of the Leader:

1. Help members work out logistics so all peer counselors can be at the elementary school on time and leave so they do not miss classtime other than peer counseling period.
2. Direct the peer counselors who are group leaders to provide the written plans to the elementary school principal, counselor, and teacher so they have the opportunity to make revisions as they wish.

Future Sessions

Procedure of the Leader:

1. Observe the peer counselors as they lead groups of elementary school students.
2. Ask peer counselors to share their feelings, successes, and list the changes they would make for future meetings with the children.
3. Ask peer counselors to evaluate this experience in terms of their evaluations from the children, the comments from elementary school teachers and the principal, and their own feelings having been a group leader.

Evaluation

Frenza (1985) indicates that the evaluation process of peer counselors should be included in the initial program design and measure the effects of the program on peer counselors, on the population being served, and on the climate of the school.

This evaluation plan was in the original design of the program, and lends itself to evaluating individual sessions. The effects of the program on the peer counselors and on the elementary children can be measured but it is extremely difficult to measure a climate of a school, furthermore, there are many variables that determine the climate of the school.

Sessions 1 and 2: A written list of common concerns of sixth grade students.

Sessions 3 and 4: Individual members' lists and discussion of the stages of group process and written entries in journals. Discussion of own individual progress in the group process.

Session 5: Written journal entries that are a summary of guidelines for group work with elementary students.

Session 6: Written goal statements for working with elementary students.

Sessions 7 and 8: Written group proposals for work with elementary students.

Session 9: Evaluation of materials and the role play. Necessary changes made.

Session 10: Journal entries and discussion about the peer counselors' growth while developing this program.

Session 11: Implementation of the group counseling program at the elementary school.

The peer counselors have considered this experience one of the highlights of the year. The only negative comments from them have been that the interaction is too short. With the addition of a full-time elementary school counselor, the peer counselors expanded the program to include additional topics. Some groups were co-led by a peer counselor and the elementary school counselor.

A high school freshman, referring to his experience with the high school peer counselor when he was in the sixth grade, provided an excellent evaluation when he said: "With the help we got from the peer counselors, going to the intermediate school was easy. I had no problems at all because I knew what would happen."

REFERENCES

Canfield, Jack & Wells, Harold C.: *100 Ways to Enhance Self-Concept in the Classroom.* Englewood Cliffs, Prentice-Hall, 1976.

Corey, Gerald and Corey, Marianne: *Groups: Process and Practice* (3rd Ed.). Monterey, Brooks/Cole, 1987.

D'Andrea, Vincent & Salovey, Peter: *Peer Counseling Skills and Perspectives.* Palo Alto, Science and Behavior, 1983.

Delworth, U., and Brown, W. F.: The paraprofessional as a member of the college guidance team. In Frenza, 1985.

Frenza, Mary: Peer counseling. *Highlights, an ERIC/CAPS Fact Sheet.* Ann Arbor, Education Resources Information Center, 1985.

Huey, Wayne C.: Informational-processing groups: A peer-led orientation approach. *The School Counselor.* September 1985.

Myrick, Robert D. & Erney, Tom.: *Caring and Sharing: Becoming a Peer Facilitator.* Minneapolis, Educational Media Corp., 1978.

Myrick, Robert D. & Erney, Tom: *Youth Helping Youth: A Handbook for Training Peer Facilitators.* Minneapolis, Educational Media, 1979.

Ratliffe, Sharon & Herman, Deldd: *Self-Awareness.* Lincolnwood, National Textbook, 1982.

Simon, Sidney: *Meeting Yourself Halfway.* Niles, Argus, 1974.

Tindall, Judith, & Gray, H. Dean: *Peer Power, Becoming An Effective Peer Helper.* Muncie, Accelerated Development, 1985.

Chapter Eleven

PREVENT SUBSTANCE ABUSE

HELP STUDENTS STAY SOBER

Dorothy J. Scrivner Blum

Rationale

The personal and social damage that substance abuse inflicts on young people compels schools to develop new strategies for treatment and prevention (Lachance, 1984). Schools have tried to prevent abuse of alcohol and other drugs in three ways: (1) educating students about the physical and mental hazards of using alcohol and other drugs, (2) suspending and/or expelling students who have paraphernalia and/or are using or are under the influence of alcohol or other drugs on school grounds, (3) notifying police or using police on campus. These methods do not address the underlying problems, but attempt to treat the symptoms. Young people have not been deterred from experimenting and/or using drugs at private parties during week-ends or vacations. A report conducted by the National Parents' Resource Institute for Drug Education (PRIDE, 1988), confirms that fewer than 2 percent of the students said they use alcohol, marijuana or cocaine in school. The results of a study conducted by PRIDE in 1987–88 show that students from twenty-four states in grades six through twelve "overwhelmingly" use drugs in social settings on weekends and, to a lesser extent, on weekday evenings. Three of ten high school students who drank liquor said they usually become "very high" or "bombed" when they do. It is alarming that within the past year (1987–88) high school seniors reported to PRIDE that 64 percent drank beer, 64 percent drank wine coolers, 54 percent drank liquor, 25 percent used marijuana, 8 percent used uppers, 5 percent used cocaine, and 4 percent used downers, hallucinogens or inhalants. Young people who drink or use other drugs report doing so at friends' homes, in their cars, or in their own homes.

The level of drug abuse among young people in the United States is the highest of any developed country of the world (Lachance, 1984). Many children who are into heavy drugs by the age of seventeen have started by age eleven (Lachance, 1984).

Schools must provide methods to make it popular and the "in-thing" *not* to use alcohol and other drugs. Peer influence is strong during adolescence. Furthermore, young people are quick to recognize and discount hypocritical adults who insist that it is wrong for young people to abuse drugs, when these same adults abuse alcohol. The high school chapters of Students Against Drunk Driving (SADD) have saved numerous lives by emphasizing the dangers of drinking and driving, and adult groups have provided drivers to and from proms. However, some student members of these groups state that it's O.K. to drink, just don't drive when you drink alcohol. "Just Say No" groups popularize the idea that it is not smart to drink alcohol or abuse other drugs. Alcoholics Anonymous sponsors dances and parties for young people. Young recovering abusers of alcohol or other drugs find it comfortable socializing with others who are trying to abstain. They have a common interest and support system while beginning or maintaining a social life.

Group counseling offers the opportunity for previous substance abusers to learn that their concerns are not unique. They frequently deny, blame, and rationalize to excuse their behaviors. A group of peers in which other previous abusers recognize and confront these defenses is more likely to get the young person to recognize his/her denial, than an adult individual counselor alone (Lachance, 1984). This group offers confrontation and support accompanied with understanding and caring.

Swaim (1987) found that anger has a significant correlation with adolescent drug use. Previous drug abusing students need a safe place to vent anger toward their peers, siblings, parents, teachers, and others. Only after venting their anger are they able to accept that they cannot change another person, that they can change only their own reactions to and interactions with other people.

These students can be highly critical of others. Group counseling helps them begin to accept that they, too are imperfect human beings, but they are worth-while and deserving of self-dignity and self-respect, regardless of what they have done in the past. As they learn to respect themselves and become more self-confident, they begin to respect others and not demand that others always treat them fairly and be perfect. It takes a secure, self-assured person to respond with dignity when being treated unfairly.

As Binion, et al (1988) found, adolescents take drugs for social reasons and because drugs make them feel good, but the more seriously drug involved young people say they take drugs when they are anxious, depressed, or alienated. In many cases these young people have resorted to alcohol or other drugs to escape painful feelings. These teen-agers often experience family conflicts, lack self-esteem, and have strong feelings of anger.

The social lives of high school students frequently revolve around week-end parties with alcohol or other drugs. When a young person is trying to abstain from all drugs it can be lonely because this person is told in group that he/she must create a new social life, and usually this means making new friends. As a result, old friends may call the straight person weird and may ridicule him/her. Although the abstaining young person may want desperately to make friends with students who do not drink, the non-drinkers cannot be sure of the previous drug-abuser, and the non-drinking students do not want to get involved. They may be fearful of the previous drug-abuser. Therefore it is lonely for the person who is making an attempt to not use drugs. In group this is discussed and members relate the pain they felt when they left their old group without knowing anyone else, yet knowing they had to do it for their own good. Often group members help others socially by talking about drug-free places where young people get together and sometimes offering rides to each other.

These students are like other adolescents, characterized by paradoxes. They push and test limits, yet recognize and appreciate limits as a sign of caring. They are self-centered, yet very sensitive of others' feelings. They try and often succeed in looking hard and cold, yet they are vulnerable and easily hurt. They say they don't care how others treat them but they are desperate for positive recognition and acceptance from others.

Definition of this Group

Members of this group must want to abstain from alcohol and other drug use. The group began in 1986 with students who returned to school from various substance abuse treatment programs. Gradually these members recommended the group experience to friends who were abusing drugs but said they wanted to quit. Members, who said that the group supported them in remaining sober, asked the leader to interview these friends so they could join the group. Students were not permitted to attend the group without individual interviews with the leader.

Males and females at grade levels nine through twelve were members in this group, and they continued as members for as long as they needed this support to remain drug-free. The leaders expected the group to meet only one semester, but members asked to continue and the leaders extended the group for the entire school year. The first week of the following school year, five previous members asked a leader if the group could resume for the new school year, and requested that they continue to be members of the group. The leaders suggested privately to three members that they were ready and strong enough to abstain on their own, and maintain a drug-free life-style. However, in each case, the student asked to continue with the group to work on other issues. The leaders granted permission and these members worked on family and school issues until they graduated one year later.

Leaders

Co-leaders of this group were the school guidance director and the school social worker. Because such a group can get very intense with many complex family problems, it is wise to co-lead this group. One leader can observe the members while the other leads and participates in the group. Also, when one leader must be out of the building on the date of a session, the other leader meets with the group. These co-leaders must have similar philosophies of counseling, of the group process, and of drug abuse. They must trust each other's intent and skills implicitly. They must both be astute, open, accepting, non-judgmental, willing to share their own deep, personal feelings, experiences, and personal values. They must be empathic, listen attentively, perceive feelings, interpret statements of feeling, be willing to take well calculated risks, and respect ideas, values and feelings different from their own. Leaders should have experience leading structured groups before leading this particular group. Before offering such a group in a school, it is important that a successful group program exists with non-threatening group seminars and other groups. Otherwise students feel identified as "druggies" and students and faculty view group counseling as being only for students who have serious problems.

Screening Interview

The interviewing counselor accepted the potential member's desire to be free of drugs and was non-judgmental of the applicant and his/her friends. During the interview, the leader ascertained the extent to which he/she believed the person would accept responsibility to change his/her drug-abusing life-style, and the extent to which this potential member would help other members in the group. During the screening interview some potential members decided the group was not for them, and in other cases the leader told the applicants that she did not believe they were ready to make the kind of commitment required of group members. In all cases the leader and candidates continued to respect each other and the offer remained open if, at a later time, the applicants wanted to talk with the leader again. One candidate did this, convinced the leader he was ready to make the commitment, and was a productive and committed member in the group.

Questions asked at this screening interview include:

1. How long has it been since your last use of alcohol or other drugs?
2. Which drugs did you use?
3. Have you been through a treatment program?
4. What program? What were the results? What was helpful about the program?
5. How did you find out about this group?
6. Why do you want to be a member of this group?
7. How would you change your social life to remain free of alcohol and other drugs?
8. What do you enjoy doing with friends when not drinking or using drugs?
9. Have you attended Alcoholics Anonymous or a similar group? Have you attended their social events? How did you feel about attending these meetings?
10. Have you ever before been asked to keep information in confidence? How did you respond?
11. If you attended this group for three sessions, would you keep the names and information confidential, even if you decided after that time not to join the group?
12. What may I (the leader) share with the group about you and your desire to join the group and abstain from drug abuse? May I give the members of the group your name if they keep that in confidence?

13. I will tell the group that you wish to join, and I will tell them the things you have given me permission to share with them. May I also tell them what I have said to you in terms of the way I see your commitment to change?

The applicants were told: "After attending three sessions you will be asked to either make a commitment to the group, or terminate. In either case you must keep names and information confidential. Who attends this group or why is nobody else's business."

Goals

- Help members abstain from alcohol and other drugs, not only during school hours but during vacations and week-ends as well.
- Provide a support group where members feel accepted, and can express themselves freely in a non-judgmental atmosphere.

Procedure

Although both leaders had led structured groups in the past, this group was unstructured. Members could talk about anything that was bothering them. They had so many issues that they wanted to discuss that a member requested that there be priority at the beginning of each group session, so members with the most pressing problems of the week could get help from the group. This suggestion was followed. Members of this group were coping with serious family and social issues. Confidentiality prevents revealing specific information. Counseling skill is crucial to deal with such intense issues and a beginning counselor may want to co-lead this kind of group with an experienced group leader.

When asked direct questions, the leaders responded honestly and/or asked other members for their ideas. This encouraged members to be confident that their ideas were important too, not just the leaders'. The leaders were not judgmental about others outside of the group, or the members. They were supportive of various treatment programs and encouraged members to attend. Frequently members gave each other rides to Alcoholics Anonymous meetings and dances.

Members gained in their ability to help others. They were confrontive and expected honesty and commitment from other members. When they doubted this, they confronted members in the group.

From time to time a member admitted drinking, getting drunk, or using drugs. The leaders and other members expressed regret but listened attentively as the member painfully related the antecedents, the situation, the loss of self-control, and the results. A leader or member then would ask the member how he/she would prevent the same thing from happening again. Responsibility was always put upon the young people to make decisions that they knew were right for them. Leaders and members expressed appreciation for the honesty and forthrightness of members who had the courage to tell the group that they had let themselves and the group down, but the group was there to help them, not to cast blame. Members were told that all of us at sometime do things that we regret. During the sessions from time to time, members were asked to give the number of days they had "been straight—without any substance."

Frequently the bell rang for the next class period before the session had reached conclusion. The group knew, at that time, to take each others' hands around the circle and one person would recite the confidentiality pledge in his/her own words. "We will not reveal to any person what was said here because we trust each other and want the best for each other."

Teacher Support

Teachers were supportive of this group because they could see the members working for their own and others' sobriety. The leaders told members that their teachers knew that they were members in the group and were informed of the goals for the group. One leader always informed the teachers in writing of the members' attendance each session. The second year of this group all weekly sessions had to be fourth period so all members could attend. Admittedly, this made it easier for the group leaders because they only had to inform one teacher for each member.

Evaluation

Regrettably, the leaders did not design a written evaluation for the members to complete anonymously. Members continually told the leaders and other members that they felt the group was worthwhile. The record of the days of sobriety reported each week would have been an objective measure compared with the baseline of their drug involvement before membership in the group. The leaders did not keep a written record of this, believing this was information only for the group members. During the two years that this group met, all members who were seniors graduated from high school. This is viewed as an accomplishment because teachers expressed doubt that these students without the support of this group, could have continued in school.

REFERENCES

Adams, Ron. Drug-free schools are a reality, with most abuse occurring off campus. *Education Daily.* Dec. 21, 1988. National Parents' Resource Institute for Drug Education (PRIDE). The Hurt Building, 50 Hurt Plaza, Suite 210, Atlanta, GA 30303.

Binion, A., Miller, D. C., Beauvais, F., & Oetting, E. R.: Rationales for the use of alcohol, marijuana, and other drugs by eighth grade Native American and Anglo youth. *International Journal of the Addictions. 23,* 47–64, 1988.

Lachance, Laurie. Adolescent substance abuse: Counseling issues. *In Brief* An Information Digest from Educational Resources Information Center Counseling and Personnel Services. Ann Arbor, School of Education, University of Michigan. 1984.

Oetting, Eugene R. & Beauvais, Fred: Adolescent drug use and the counselor. *The School Counselor. 36,* September 1988.

Swaim, R.: Links from emotional distress to adolescent drug use: A path model. Dissertation, Colorado State University, 1987, In Oetting & Beauvais, 1988.

Chapter Twelve

PREVENT DROPOUTS

WHO AM I?

THELMA NICHOLS CALBERT

Rationale

"To reveal myself openly and honestly takes the rawest kind of courage. If I tell you who I am, you may not like who I am, and it is all that I have." (Jersild, 1957). Young people's behavior and performance reflect how they feel about themselves. A positive self-image is crucial to succeed academically in school or ultimately in life. The prerequisite for developing a strong and positive self-image is to know oneself, accept oneself, control oneself, like oneself, have courage and confidence in oneself and ultimately to have self-worth.

Our society demands that almost every adult get at least a high school education. A growing share of entry-level jobs require more skills, not less, yet every year 700,000 young Americans drop out of school (Cordtz, 1989).

Both the student and society lose when a student drops out of school. The individual loses purchasing power and society loses taxes. Dropouts have inadequate personal skills, undeveloped cognitive skills, lower lifetime earnings, and higher rates of unemployment. Welfare rolls are predominantly dropouts. Unemployment rates are high among high school dropouts and other costs to society include lowered productivity, less-skilled employees, expensive social services, and a greater liklihood of crime by dropouts (Green & Baker, 1987).

Larsen and Shertzer (1987) state that police statistics show that unemployed dropouts are six to ten times more likely than employed adults to get involved in crime. Conant (1961) suggested that the dropout problem represented "social dynamite." Society is hostile to dropouts who do not take advantage of the free education provided. This reinforces the dropouts' feelings of worthlessness (Beck & Muia, 1980).

Potential dropouts usually can be identified as students who:

- Were retained in the early grades.
- Have parents who dropped out of school.
- Come from a lower socio-economic class.
- Are Black or Hispanic.
- Have a record of truancy or excessive absence from class.
- Do not participate in school activities.
- Have low or failing grades in two or more academic courses.
- Do not communicate well.
- Demonstrate little interest in classroom work.

Hicks (1969), as cited in Larsen & Shertzer, 1987, described the steps that dropouts seem to follow. They (1) lose interest in school, (2) get lower grades, (3) skip classes, (4) get into conflicts with school authorities, (5) act out frustrations in classes or school, (6) get suspended as a result of their misbehavior, (7) get into conflicts with their parents when the parents are contacted by school authorities, and (8) eventually quit school.

When dropouts were asked why they decided to leave high school, they consistently cited four major reasons (Beekman, 1988; Curley, Sawyer, & Savitsky, 1971; "Dade County High School," 1984; "Philadelphia High School," 1977; Kumar & Bergstrand, 1979; Anon., 1982; Norris, Wheeler & Finley, 1980; Peng & Takai, 1983).

- A dislike of school and a view that school is boring and not relevant to their needs.
- Low academic achievement, poor grades, or academic failure.
- A need for money and a desire to work full-time.
- Pregnancy or marriage.

Researchers gave the same basic reasons, but were specific in providing details about the reasons dropouts don't stay in school. They stated that:

- A dislike of school is related to high absenteeism and little, if any, participation in extracurricular activities.
- Low academic achievement is likely when students have low performance in either reading or mathematics in elementary school.
- Families of low socio-economic status tend to perpetuate dropouts. These families may need the money dropouts provide even though they are low-paying jobs.

- Pregnancy or marriage may be related to the dislike of school, low academic achievement, or low self-esteem.

The dropout usually has low self-esteem, little desire for self-growth, and limited commitment to accepted social values. Frequently he/she feels inadequate, does not have friends, is not interested in extracurricular activities, and sees no purpose in continuing school. However, dropouts often are intelligent (Howard & Anderson, 1978, Elliott, Voss, & Wendling, 1966, Sewell, Palmo, & Manni, 1981, as cited in Larsen & Shertzer, 1987).

Larsen and Shertzer (1987) maintain that school counselors should promote the self-confidence and self-worth of potential dropouts. These authors suggest that school counselors: (1) identify potential dropouts, and (2) plan support programs for these identified dropouts. "An effective way to work with these high risk students seems to be in small groups of six to ten members" (Larsen & Shertzer, 1987, p. 167). Through group participation, potential dropouts learn that other students also have difficulty in adjusting to school, and that members can support each other and provide suggestions to resolve problems (Larsen & Shertzer, 1987).

Goals

The purpose for this group is to help potential dropouts gain in their feelings of self-worth and self-confidence in school. It is believed that by feeling better about themselves and knowing that other members and the leader care about them, these potential dropouts will find school a more pleasant place where they can learn to be successful.

The goals for this group are for each member to:

- Describe one positive "self-talk message" that he/she can use when the going gets tough.
- List two strengths that he/she acknowledges he/she has.
- List two goals related to school work that he/she will try to accomplish next quarter.

Definition of the Group

This group is designed for identified potential dropouts during their first semester of the ninth grade because succeeding in this grade level is one of the biggest educational challenges for students. They are changing developmentally from children into adolescents and are changing their focus from seeking adult approval to seeking peer approval. They also are moving from a small, protective educational environment to a large, often rather impersonal school. High school teachers frequently are more subject-oriented than student-oriented and often there is no homeroom. It is easy to get lost socially and left behind academically.

The group meets once a week for six weeks. The sessions last one class period and the meetings alternate each week so members miss each class only once.

Selection of Members

The counselor identifies potential dropouts from the eighth grade students; those who have been retained, who have excessive absences, who are not involved in school activities, and who have low and/or failing grades. After making a list of these students, the counselor talks with teachers and other adults who know the students. Efforts are made to avoid the neighborhood effect, having dating couples, and/or best friends in the same group. The counselor speaks individually to each potential member to learn if he/she would be interested in joining a small support group. Two role models, students who were absent a lot or retained, but now are succeeding in school, are asked if they are interested in helping others, and in return, get support for the academic changes they have made. A total of six to ten students are in this group. Parents are contacted personally, and are told that this group is a support group to help their children like school and get more out of school.

Procedures

Each session is introduced with an activity that focuses on some aspect of self. Discussion follows the exercise. The procedures are designed to help members feel worthwhile and to help these potential dropouts assess their direction. The group is an opportunity for these members to share their experiences and feelings about themselves and have the opportunity to see how other group members see them. It is expected that by sharing experiences and feelings, members will become more aware of the expectations at school, and find school a more comfortable and welcome place to be.

Students are not judged right or wrong about the conclusions they draw, their biases and prejudices, or the reasons they think the way they do, but they are challenged by other viewpoints. They are given the opportunity to state what they think and feel, as long as they don't hurt another member in the group. A subsequent group may be held the following semester to further pursue academic progress and focus more specifically on attendance, completing school work on time, and raising school achievement. (See Chapter One).

Sessions

Session 1—Get Acquainted

Purpose: Help members get acquainted with each other and develop a spirit of trust and acceptance.

Procedure of the Counselor:

1. Introduce all members to each other.
2. Ask each member in the circle to give his/her name and tell something he/she likes to do. They try to act it out. The second time around the circle, members recite everyone else's name and what they said they like to do.
3. Tell the members that the purpose of the group is to help each other develop self-confidence and succeed in high school. "Sometimes in a large school it is easy to get lost and feel that you don't know anyone. Members in the group will help each other to find the positive or good things about themselves."
4. Read aloud and explain the "Rules for Group Members" which are posted on the wall.
    - I will participate in the group as fully as I can. I must not be absent because it hurts the group when I do not share the experiences of the group.
    - I will not belittle myself or others.
    - I will not probe, or analyze other people. The group is to help me become more aware of myself and learn to appreciate others.
    - I will express my thoughts, feelings, attitudes and behaviors as I become aware of them. As I share, others will discover and get to know me.

- I will not talk about people outside the group. I will take responsibility for my behavior and will not blame others.
5. Also review and post the "Rules for Group Discussions."
    - Always speak for yourself, not for someone else. Say, "I think...," not "We, he, she, they, or some people think...."
    - When speaking of someone in the group, speak directly to him/her. Instead of saying "John over there...," say, "You, John...."
    - Make statements outright instead of phrasing statements like questions. Instead of saying "Who cares?" say "I feel that no one cares." Questions sometimes shift the emphasis from yourself to another person. Keep the emphasis on yourself. Say what you think or how you feel.
    - Speak in the present tense. Feelings are sometimes lost by expressing them in the past tense. Do not say, "I thought" or "I felt" but rather, "I think" or "I feel." This will make you more aware of your own feelings and better able to communicate them to others.
    - Do not use cop outs. Some phrases are used to avoid seeing or expressing true feelings. Some common examples are "I don't know." (Can mean "I don't want to know.") "Don't ask me." (Can mean "You'll be mad if I tell you.") "I can't" (Can mean "I don't want to.") "That's the way it is." (Can mean "I won't do anything about it.") and "What can I say?" (Can mean "Stop picking on me.")
6. Give directions for another activity. It is called "Merry-Go-Round." Do the activity first by saying, "My favorite food is... because...." The next person will also give a favorite food and the reason, until all in the circle have responded with their favorite food.
7. Close the session by expressing pleasure that all could be there and that you, the counselor, expect to see them all _____ period next _____ day. Tell them that hall-passes will be provided and teachers will be informed.

Session 2—Self-Revelation

Purpose: Help each member reveal something new about him/her-self to other members of the group.

Procedure of the Counselor:

1. Going around the circle, finish this sentence: "If I could be any television personality I could, I would choose to be (name the person), because...." Then go around the circle and remember names of members with their favorite television personalities.
2. Remind members of the rules for group discussions and ask a member to select one rule and discuss what it means.
3. Tell the members that today they will be in a "Serendipity Lab." The purpose of the lab is to help them discover who they are by revealing a little about themselves to others in their small sub-group.
4. Give the members the itinerary of the "Serendipity lab." (1) Preliminary drawing. Everyone draws something about themselves, (2) Small-group interaction. In a small group of four, each member describes their drawing, and (3) Self-revelation. Each person tells something honestly about themselves.
5. Model the activity by showing your drawing, and honestly sharing something significant about yourself.
6. Divide the group into three sub-groups of four members each. Then give directions for the lab:

Preliminary Drawing (Five minutes) Ask everyone in silence, to select four crayons to represent the four dominant colors in his/her life. "Draw on the paper a symbol for each major part of your life. For instance, if athletics is a major influence in your life, you might draw a football. If money is a major concern, you might draw a dollar sign."

Small Group Interaction (Twelve to fifteen minutes) Ask members to describe their drawings and what their drawings mean to them. Other members may ask questions and the artists may answer questions about their drawings if they wish. At this time the artists do not reveal the reason the drawings represent important aspects of their lives. Each person has three minutes.

Self-Revelation (Twelve to fifteen minutes) Each person now reveals *why* each symbol is important to him/her. How did he/she begin to become interested in it? How important is it now? Was another person influential in this aspect of his/her life? Tell members that they may answer questions when they wish.

7. Bring the entire group together for the summary.
8. Summarize the session by asking each member to tell the entire group about one drawing of their own, and one drawing of another

person in their small group. That person has the right to correct or revise anything said about his/her drawing.
9. Link drawings together and remind members of the confidentiality between sessions.
10. Remind members that group will meet _____ period next week.

Session 3—Self-Concept

Purpose: Help members learn to give and accept sincere compliments.

Procedure of the Counselor:

1. Review the last session. Ask members to remember important aspects that other members revealed. Tell them that members took risks to tell about themselves, and only when we can be assured of trust of other members, can we afford to take meaningful risks.
2. Prepare the members for the next activity. Stress that there is something good about everyone. Ask members the following questions: (1) What is a self-concept? (2) How is it formed? (3) Can it be changed? (4) How can it be changed? (5) Can we influence each other's self-concept? (6) How does a sincere compliment make you feel? (7) How do you react to a sincere compliment?

   Ask members to write the name of each student in the group and write one honest, positive statement about that person's relationships with other people. Include the counselor's name and their own.

   Tape a blank piece of paper to each member's back. Give each member a felt-tip pen, for writing only on the papers that are taped to the backs of members.

   Ask students to write a positive comment on the papers on the backs of all other members. After all papers have a positive comment, ask each person to remove his/her sheet, read it to the entire group and accept the compliments graciously. Some members may need help to say, "Thank you," or "I appreciate that comment." No member is to deny any statement.

   Encourage members to take their papers home or to their lockers, tape them where they can see them every day and acknowledge that these are honest compliments.

3. Summarize the session by giving a definition of self-concept, and remind members of the time and period of the next meeting.

Session 4—Self-Talk

Purpose: Help members learn about self-talk, stressing that we need to tell ourselves that we are O.K. It is not conceited to acknowledge our strengths.

Procedure of the Counselor:
1. Summarize the last session. Go around the circle, each person giving one compliment that he/she received last week, and graciously thanking the person who gave it.
2. Stress that sometimes others may see our good points but we don't allow ourselves to admit them. In this session we are going to give ourselves messages to acknowledge our strengths and make us feel good after we receive a "Strength Bombardment."
3. Distribute papers and pencils and ask members to put their names in the upper right hand corner and circle them. Members are to think of one thing that they do well. They are to write this in the middle of a sheet of paper and draw a circle around it. Then they pass their papers to the right and other members add strengths that they honestly believe this person shows. Papers are returned to the people whose names are in the upper right hand corners. Members read aloud the strengths on their papers as they speak clearly, hold their heads high, and establish eye contact with other members. Admittedly, this is hard to do when talking about yourself, but it is important to practice.
4. Summarize the positive things that have been said and suggest that now they can admit that they do these things well.
5. Describe self-talk as messages that we tell ourselves and that influence our behavior. Frequently our self-talk is negative. Ask members to list put-downs we may give ourselves, and then list them on newsprint for all to see. Draw an X through these negative messages. Declare that from now on, members will not give each other nor themselves put-downs. Members pledge this in the group.
6. Ask members to think of positive self-talk to take the place of negative self-talk. These are messages that are honest but also make us feel good. List these on newsprint. Brainstorm a long list.

7. Ask members to select three self-talk messages that they will tell themselves three times during the next week. Members write these three messages on a card and carry the card in their pockets or purses throughout the seven days until the next meeting.
8. Ask members not to leave until they have written the three messages to carry each day.

Session 5—Self-Inventory

Purpose: Help members disclose more about themselves, and admit their strengths.
Materials: Questions on slips of paper, folded, to be drawn from a hat.

Procedure of the Counselor:
1. Ask members if they used the positive self-talk. Ask them when and how they used the messages on the card. Stress that we must constantly remind ourselves of the things we do well.
2. Introduce the activity, "Self-Inventory." Members take turns being the volunteer focus person in this activity. The focus person sits in the middle of the circle and answers the questions as honestly as possible, or passes if he/she does not want to answer that question. Other members draw questions from a hat and they ask these questions in the order of the numbers. After the first focus person, the questions are mixed up, and re-distributed.
   Questions for the Self-Inventory.
   (1) What was the happiest year or period in your life?
   (2) Tell about a turning point in your life.
   (3) What self-talk is most helpful to you?
   (4) What things do you do well?
   (5) Was there a time when you showed exceptional courage?
   (6) What are some things you would like to do better?
   (7) What would you like to improve in your school work?
   (8) Who could help you with your school work?
   (9) Describe a time when you felt really great, a peak experience.
   (10) Tell about a missed opportunity.
3. Ask a member to summarize the session. Remind members that the next session is the final session.

Session 6—New Goals

Purpose: Members evaluate the group experience and set new personal goals.

Procedure of the Counselor:

1. Finish the self-inventory so each member has a chance to be the focus person.
2. Review that the purpose of this group was to help each other develop self-confidence and succeed in high school.
3. Ask each member to think of three personal goals related to school work that he/she would like to accomplish this semester. It could be to improve attendance, grades, or homework, but should be realistic and within the person's power to accomplish it. Ask each member to write these three goals and the date on a card.
4. Ask each member to look at his/her goals and answer the questions:
   - Can I do this on my own without someone else doing something for me?
   - Do I want to achieve this goal this semester?
   - What will be most difficult for me?
   - How can I overcome any barriers?
   - Will I try hard to achieve it?
5. Ask members to read aloud their goals related to school work and leave them with you. You will make a copy and give copies to them later. Ask if you have their permission to share their goals with their teacher(s).
6. Ask members to complete the evaluation form (12-1).
7. Tell members that the group will meet again to review their progress on their school related goals at the end of the quarter, and then again at the end of the semester.

Session 7—Review of Academic Progress Two Weeks After the Group Has Ended

Review goals and progress. Congratulate those who have achieved their goals. Work with those who have not yet achieved their goals.

Collect information about the members' school performance during their last semester of eighth grade and compare this with their performance during the first semester of the ninth grade. Compare the following:

- Attendance. Number of days present.
- Tardiness. Number of class tardies.
- Office visits. Number of times sent to the office from class because of misbehavior.
- Suspensions. Number of in-house suspensions as well as number of days of out-of-school suspensions.

If the group seemed to work well together and benefit from the support, they may continue to meet the next quarter to raise their academic achievement, using the proposal in the first chapter.

Appendix 12-1

EVALUATION

Directions: Complete the questions as completely as you can.
1. Write one example of "positive self-talk" that you can tell yourself when the going gets tough.
   _____
   _____

2. -3. List two strengths that group members noticed and that you acknowledge that you have.
   _____
   _____

4. -5. List two goals related to school work that you will try to accomplish next quarter.
   _____
   _____

REFERENCES

Anon.: *Mother Got Tired of Taking Care of My Baby: A Study of Dropouts.* Austin, Austin Independent School District, 1982.

Beck, L., & Muia, J.: The portrait of a tragedy: Research findings on the dropout. *High School Journal, 64:*65–72, 1980.

Beekman, Nancy: The dropout's perspective on leaving school. *CAPS Camsule.* Ann Arbor: Educational Resources Information Center/Counseling and Personnel Services. Nos. 2 & 3, 1988.

Conant, J. B.; *Slums and Suburbs.* N.Y., McGraw-Hill, 1961.

Cordtz, Dan: Dropouts: Retrieving America's labor lost. *Financial World.* 36–46. April 4, 1989.

Curley, T. J., Sawyer, A. P. & Savitsky, A. J.: *A Critical Analysis of School Leavers in the Quincy Public School System. (1969-1970).* Quincy, Quincy Public Schools, 1971.

Elliott, D., Voss, H., & Wendling, A.: Capable dropouts and the social milieu of high school. *Journal of Educational Research, 60,* 180–186, 1966.

Green, K. R. & Baker, A.: *Promising Practices for High-risk Youth in the Northwest Region: Initial Search.* Portland, Northwest Regional Educational Lab, Education and Work Program, 1986.

Hicks, J.: All's calm in the crows nest. *American Education, 5,* 9–10, 1969.

High School Drop Outs and the Inner City. Final Report of the Grand Jury in the Circuit Court of the Eleventh Judicial Circuit of Florida In and For the County of Dade. Miami: Dade County Grand Jury, 1984.

High School Dropouts: Highlight Results of a Survey of Philadelphia Public High School Pupils Who Left School in 1975-76. Philadelphia, Philadelphia School District, 1977.

Howard, M. A. & Anderson, R.: Early identification of potential school dropouts: A literature review. *Child Welfare, 57:* 221–231, 1978.

Jersild, Arthur T.: *The Psychology of Adolescence.* N.Y., Macmillan, 1957.

Kumar, V., & Bergstrand, J.: *Follow-Up of High School Non-Completers, 1967-1976.* Madison, University of Wisconsin, 1979.

Larsen, Pam & Shertzer, Bruce: The high school dropout: Everybody's problem? *Chronicle Guidance.* Monrovia, Chronicle Guidance Publications. February. 1988.

Norris, C., Wheeler, L, & Finley, M. J.: *Special Report: The Dropout Problem.* Phoenix, Phoenix Union High School District, 1980.

Peng, S. S: & Takai, R. T.: *High School Dropouts: Descriptive Information From 'High School and Beyond.'* Washington, D. C., National Center for Education Statistics, 1983.

Sewell, T., Palmo, A. & Manni, J.: High school dropout: Psychological, academic, and vocational factors. *Urban Education, 16,* 65–76, 1981.

INDEX

A

Abilities,
    personal, 98, 104
    questionnaire, 112–113
Ability, definition of, 101
About Me, questionnaire, 128, 134
Abstinence, alcohol/drug, 149–156
Academic,
    grades, 3–21, 23, 35, 36, 41, 42, 47, 56, 65, 117, 143, 158–160, 167–168
Acceptance, 116, 130
Achievement,
    group goal, xvii (*see* Group sessions, planned)
    school, 3–21, 23, 34, 35, 36, 41–54, 116, 161, 166, 167, 168
Activities (*see* Icebreakers, Energizers)
    age appropriate, 143, 145
    follow-up, 118
    get acquainted, 43, 58, 59, 60, 61, 62
    get acquainted, 127, 135–136
    guided fantasy, 82, 86
Activity,
    body relaxation, 51
    brainstorming, 29
    combination locks, 146
    communication exercise, 9
    Connect the Dots, 6, 17
    Dinner Table, 69
    Effective Communication, 10–11
    Empty Chair, 119
    Expanded Name Tag, 5
    Family Sculpture, 70
    Family Tree, 69
    Four Corners, Personal Feelings, 8
    Funniest Thing, 43
    Future Projection, 31
    Get Acquainted Bingo, 49, 68

Get Acquainted Interview, 26
Get Acquainted Name Game, 43, 58, 59, 60, 61, 62, 97, 116, 161
Getting to Know You, 127, 135–136
Goal Achievement, 130
Goal Setting, 5–6, 68, 70, 127, 128
Here and Now Face, 131
Hope Chest, 12, 20, 31, 73, 134
I Got Rhythm, 11
I Learned Statements, 16–17, 99, 107–108, 119
I Message, 118
Identification of Feelings, 71
Important Person, 163
Introduction, 97
Listening Skill, 12
Magic Box, 10
Merry-Go-Round, 162
Name Game, 43, 58, 59, 60, 61, 62, 97, 116
Perfection Bingo, 36
Positive Feelings, 128–129
Positive Statements, 164–165
Pre-Exam Activity, 46
Process Information, 18
Projective Drawing, 71
Recall Names, 69
Recognizing Prejudices, 132–133
Role Reversal, 131, 138–139
Satisfying Learning Experiences, 19
Self-Inventory, 166
Serendipity Lab, 163
Strength Bombardment, 62, 119, 129
Test-Taking Activity, 48
Trust Walk, 131
Values Auction, 98–99, 105–107
Way Out, 7
Whom Do I Wish to be Like?, 26, 27
Writing, 83
Adam and Me, poem, 28, 37

171

Adams, R., 149, 156
Adderholdt-Elliott, M., 27, 34, 35, 38
Administration, support of, xviii, 73
Administrators, school, 60
Admissions counselors, college, 80, 82
Admissions, college (*see* College, admissions)
Adolescents,
    concerns of, 3, 13, 23-24, 34-37, 41-42, 50-51, 55-56, 63-64, 65-66, 74-76, 79-80, 95-96, 117-120, 123-124, 137-139, 149-151, 157-159
    development of, 55, 95, 141, 151, 160
Advocacy, parents', 67-68
Affirmation, writers's, 80, 81
Age, 95
Alcohol, abuse of, 149-156
Alcoholics Anon., 150, 153, 154
Aldridge, M., v, xxi, 65-78
Allers, R. D., 74, 75, 76, 77
Anderson, R., 159, 169
Anger, 34, 35, 65, 75-76, 104, 118, 124, 125, 150
Anon., 158, 168
Anxiety scale, 45, 50
Anxiety,
    feelings of, 41, 65, 95, 151
    levels of, 43, 44, 45, 47
    physical manifestations, 42, 44
    reduction of, 41-42
    test of, 41-58
Applicants,
    peer counseling, 143
    drug-free group, 153
Application questions, college, 91-92
Aptitude, 101, 104
    definition of, 112
    questionnaire, 112
Athletic director, 60,
Attendance,
    group, 155
    school, 57, 158, 160, 161, 167, 168
Attitudes, change of, 124, 125, 134
Auction, values, 98, 105-107
Audience, writing, 79-80
Autobiography, career, 102, 113
Awareness, career (*see* Career, awareness)

B

Baker, A., 157, 169
Baker, S. B., 65, 66, 78
Barriers,
    achieving goals and, 6, 128
    communication, 10
Bauld, H., 93
Beauvais, F., 151, 156
Beck, L., 157, 168
Beckman, N., 158, 168
Beemer, L., 18, 20
Behavioral rehearsal, stressful situations, 72, 73
Behaviors, 144, 157, 158
Bergstrand, J., 158, 169
Berkovitz, I. H., 124, 125, 140
Bibliotherapy, divorce group, 65, 66
Bingo game,
    get acquainted, 44, 49, 68
    perfectionist, 36
Binion, A., 151, 156
Blum, D. J., xi, xiii-xiv, xvii-xix, xxii, 15, 20, 36, 38, 49, 50, 52, 53, 54, 149-156
Blum, R. G., v
Body relaxation, techniques for, 51,
Book,
    divorce, 23, 28, 29,
    Gifted Kid's Survival Guide, The, 23, 28, 39,
    group work, xi
    How to Get It Together, 66, 69, 72, 73,
    writing essays, 79, 82
Bowman, R. P., xiii, xiv
Brainstorm, activity to, 29, 72, 81, 82, 85, 134
Britton, D. D., 19, 20
Brown University, 83, 91
Brown, W. F., 143, 148
Bulletins, school, 96, 126
Bureau of Census, predictions of, 65

C

Calbert, T. N., v, xxii, 157-169
Canfield, J., 126, 140, 145, 148
Career,
    awareness, 95-114
    guidance to select, 95-114
    interests, 96
    plans, 95, 96
    preparation, 95-114

Career center, 96, 100
Career cluster, 103
Career expectations, 95–114
Career packet, 97, 103
Careers,
　exploration of, 95–114
　parents', 97–98, 100–101
　select, 96, 104
　settings of, 110–111
Career skills, 96
Carlson, J., 28, 37, 38
Carlton College, 91–92
Carmichael, E., v, xxii, 141–148
Carroll, M., v, xi, xii,
Change, difficulty of, 66, 153
Characteristics, physical, 132
Cherry, N., 42, 54
Child study technique, brainstorm activity, 29–30
Class officers, 61
Class, peer counseling, 143
Classroom, presentation, 25, 81–82
Climate, school, xi
Clubs, school, 56, 58–59
Co-Leader, 115, 142, 143, 148, 151, 152, 153, 154 (*see* Group leaders)
Coach, athletic, 59–60
Cohesion, group, 68
College,
　admissions counselors, 80, 82, 83
　application essay, 79–93
　application questions, 83, 86, 91–92
　peer counselors, 142
Comments, hurtful, 133
Commitment, group, 154
Communication,
　activity of, 9, 10–11
　barriers to, 10
　facilitate, 67, 80, 118, 121, 142
　family, 81, 84, 95, 103, 104
　roadblocks to effective, 10
　counselor to parent, xix, 13–14, 25, 56, 67–68
　counselor to parent, 84, 96–98, 103–104
　counselor to teacher, xix, 14–15, 25, 155
　student-parent (*see* Communication, family)
　student to teacher, 10–12, 25, 41, 47, 52

　teacher to counselor, 42, 155
　teacher to student, 25, 57–62
　ways to facilitate, 121
Communication skills, 4, 9–10, 115, 126, 130
　lack of, 55
　role play of, 10–11
Compliment, 130, 164
Conant, J. B., 157, 168
Concerns, students', 142, 144, 150, 154
Confidentiality, xviii, 26, 115, 127, 129, 134, 143, 153, 154, 155
Conflict,
　family, 151, 158
　racial, 124
Confrontation, 150, 154
Connect the Dots, activity to, 6, 17
Connections, writing, 82, 85
Cordtz, D., 157, 168
Corey, G., 31, 38, 144, 148
Corey, M., 31, 38, 144, 148
Cornell University, 92
Counseling methods, 65
Counseling, individual, 65, 125
Counselor,
　elementary school, 141, 144, 145, 148
　secondary school, xii, xiii, xvii, xviii, 65, 79, 80, 96, 115, 116, 117, 123, 141, 151–153, 159
Counselors,
　college admissions (*see* College, admissions counselors)
　peer, 57, 141–148
Courses, secondary school, 95, 99–100
Cultural heritage, 123, 126
Curley, T. J., 158, 169

D

Dade Co., H.S., 158, 169
D'Andrea, V., 142, 148
Davis, S. D., 55, 64
de Lissovoy, V., 65, 66, 78
De-Mystify, writing, 81
Decision Making, 66, 72–73, 79, 82, 95, 96, 97, 98, 99, 103, 155
　steps in, 7, 17–18, 29
Decisions, career, 98
Definitions, groups (*see* Groups, descriptions of particular)

Delworth, U., 143, 148
Depression, feeling of, 151
Descriptions, group (see Groups, descriptions of particular)
Development, 55, 95, 141, 151, 160
    adolescent (see Adolescents, development)
Di Antonio, R., 93
Dialogue, 91
Dickey, T., 55, 56, 64
Differences, situational, 71-72
Dinkmeyer, D., 124, 140
Discrimination, racial, 124
Disorders, eating, 116
Disrespect, 123, 124
Divorce,
    dealing with, 65-78
    personal meaning of, 65-66
Dropouts,
    potential, 158, 159-160
    prevent, 157-169
Duke University, 92
Dyad interview, get acquainted, 26

E

Economy, unpredictable, 95
Education, 124, 141, 157
    levels, 96, 99, 100, 109
Elkind, D., 65, 77
Elliott, D., 159, 169
Energizers, 5, 6, 7, 8, 9, 10, 11, (see Activities, Icebreakers)
Environment, unstable, 95
Erney, T., 141, 148
ESL, 56, 126
Essay,
    college admissions, 79-93
    model for writing, 89-90
Essays,
    examples of college admissions, 90-91
    written by parents, 80
Ethnic groups, 123-140
Evaluation,
    Academic Group, 20, 21-22
    Career Group, 103, 104, 113-114
    Divorce Group, 73, 74-75, 77
    Dropout Prevention Group, 167-168
    follow-up, 77, 139-140
    Gifted Student Group, 37-38

Growth Group, 119-120, 122
Human Relations Group, 134, 139-140
individual sessions, 16-17, 33, 98, 129, 130, 131
midpoint, 33, 77, 139-140
Newcomers' Group, 61, 62-63
one month after group, 77
peer counseling project, 146, 147, 148
peer counselors, 147
personal progress, 144
Substance-Abuse Prevention Group, 155-156
Test-Anxiety Group, 48, 53-54
Writing Workshop, 88-89
Exams, quarter, 48
Excellence, perfectionism vs., 35
Expectations,
    gifted students, 23-24
    teachers', 57-62
Experiences,
    learning, 19
    students', 141, 144, 148
Extracurricular, program, 58-59, 159, 160

F

FCPS, xv
Families,
    adolescents in divorced, 65-78
    blended, 71-72, 116
    changing, 65-78
    divorced, 65-78
    positive aspects of, 66
Family,
    career sessions (see Group counseling, family)
    writing sessions, 81 (see Group counseling, family)
Family sculpting, activity of, 70
Family tension, 80
Family tree, activity of, 69
Fears, Students', 124, 142, 151
Feedback, group, 30, 33, 73 (see Evaluation, midpoint)
Feedback, peer, 85, 88, 116, 128, 131, 132
Feeling vocabulary, 75-76, 129
Feelings,
    anxiety, 46, 48, 55, 151
    hierarchy of, 46

Feelings (*continued*)
  students', xvii, 8, 24, 28, 46, 48, 55, 56, 66, 67, 68, 70-71, 73, 87, 88, 96, 115, 116, 118, 123-124, 125, 126, 127-128, 130, 131, 134, 142, 144, 146, 151, 152, 159, 161
  understanding, 71, 125
Filmstrip,
  Coping with Family Changes, 66
  family coping, 66
Finley, M. J., 158, 169
Fish, K. L., 124, 125, 140
Flyers, publicizing groups, 96, 126
Follow-up session, 13, 134, 167
Foreign language, expectations in courses of, 61
Four corners, activity of, 8
Framework, philosophical, 66
Francis, Anita, v, xxi, 55-64
Free writing, activity of, 79 (*see* Writing, free)
Freeman, L., 41, 54
Frenza, M., 141, 143, 147, 148
Freshmen, high school, 4, 25, 56, 61, 96, 116, 148, 152, 159-160
Friends, 101, 159
Fromkin, H. L., 126, 140
Future projection, activity of, 31

G

Galbraith, J., 23, 28, 38
Gaudreault, K., v, vi, xxi, 95-114
Gershenfeld, M. K., 9, 20
Get acquainted,
  activities, 43, 58, 59, 60, 61, 62, 97, 116, 135-136
  Bingo game, 49
Gifted Kids Survival Guide, 23, 28, 29
Gifted students, 23-39
  needs of, 23-24
Gillies, J., 135-136, 140
Glick, P., 65, 77
Goals,
  academic, 95
  barriers to achieving, 6, 128
  counselors', 79
  criteria for setting, 16, 127-128
  divorce group, 66-67
  group

individual personal, 3-4, 6, 68, 70, 95, 98, 105, 115, 116, 127, 128, 129, 130, 133, 134, 167-168
new student seminar, 56,
peer counseling project, 145
personal career
rank order, 70
Goal setting, 5-6, 68, 70, 127-128
  criteria for, 16
Goldberg, E. R., 55, 64
Gordon, T., 228, 122
Grade, level (*see* High School, grade nine, etc.)
Grades, academic, 3-21, 23, 35, 36, 41, 42, 47, 56, 65, 117, 143, 158, 159, 160, 167-168
Grandparents, essays about, 90-91
Gray, H. D., 141, 148
Green, B. J., 66, 70, 77
Green, K. R., 157, 169
Grief process, 55,
Ground rules, 5, 15-16, 26, 43, 57, 58, 68, 97, 126, 127
Group,
  functioning as a, 80
  growth, 117
  open, 56
Group counseling,
  advantages of, xi, 124-125, 142, 159
  assumptions about, xvii-xix
  closure, 155, 162, 167
  definition of, 31-32 (*see* Groups, descriptions)
  descriptions of groups (*see* Groups, descriptions)
  evaluation (*see* Groups, evaluation)
  goals (*see* Groups, goals)
  guidelines, xvii-xix
  member selection, xviii (*see* Group members)
  membership, xviii, 4, 42 (*see* Group members)
  model for, xix, 125
  plan for (*see* Group sessions, planned) xvii, xviii, 142, 145, 146
  poster, 13, 96, 135
  preventive, 66, 125
  procedures, xiv, xvii, xix, 154-155, 160-161
  process of, xii, 142, 144
  program, xvii-xix, 66, 152

Group counseling (*continued*)
  proposals, xvii, 142, 145, 146, 147
  rationale, xiii, 3, 23–24, 41–42, 55–56, 65–66, 79–80, 95–96, 123–125, 141–142, 149–151, 157–159
  role models, xvii, 4, 42,
  referral for (*see* Group members, referral for)
  schedule, xviii–xix, 14–15,
  screening for membersp (*see* Group members) xviii, 4–5
  secondary school, xiii
  stages, 144
  strategies, xiii
  Vietnamese, 125
Group feedback (*see* Feedback, group evaluation)
Group leader(s), 141, 151, 152, 153, 154
  experienced, 115, 152
  responsible, xvii–xviii
Group members,
  referrals for, xviii, 4, 25, 42–43, 56, 67, 151
  screening individual, 15, 25–26, 42, 43, 67, 96, 117, 125, 152–154
  selection of, 4–5, 25–26, 42, 43, 67, 96, 117, 125, 143, 151, 153–154, 160, 142, 152
Group rules (*see* Ground rules)
  facilitate communication (*see* Communication, ways)
Groups,
  children of divorce, 65
  description of particular, xiii–xiv, 4, 25, 42–43, 56, 57, 67, 80–81, 96–97, 116, 117–118, 125–126, 143, 151–152, 159–160
  evaluation of (*see* Group counseling, evaluation) xiv, xviii–xix, 20, 21–22, 37–38, 53–54, 61, 62–63, 73, 74–75, 77, 88–89, 113–114, 147–148, 155–156, 167–168
  family, 84
  goals for, xiii, xvii, xix, 3–4, 24, 42, 56, 66–67, 70, 81, 96, 116, 154, 159
  growth, 115–122
  membership selection (*see* Group members)
  planned sessions for (*see* Group sessions)
  procedures, 81–89 (*see* Group sessions)
  publicity of, 4, 13, 25, 56, 81–84, 96, 116–117, 126
  referral to (*see* Group members, referrals)
  sessions (*see* Group sessions)
  structured, 119 (*see* Group sessions)
  unstructured, 115–122
Group session,
  mini-group, 116–117
  parents', 81, 84, 97–98, 103–104
Group sessions, planned, 5–13, 26–31, 43–49, 57–62, 68–73, 84–88, 97–104, 144–148, 154–155, 160–168
Group work,
  schools, xi
  texts, xi
Growth groups,
  definition, 118, 121
  interest in, 121
Growth, personal, 88, 115, 141
Guidance,
  career, 95–114
  secondary school, xiii
Guidance director, 152
Guided fantasy, activity, 82, 86

H

Hammatt-Kavaloski, J., 66, 77
Harvard University, 83, 92
Harvill, R., 55, 56, 64
Hawley, R. C., 19, 20
Health, essentials for good, 8
Herbert, D., 95, 114
Herman, D., 145, 148
Hicks, J., 158, 169
Hierarchy,
  anxiety, 46,
  stressful situations, 46
High-risk students, new students, 55, 157, 169
High school,
  George C. Marshall, 141, 143
  grade eleven, 42, 56, 67, 79, 95, 125, 152
  grade nine, 4, 25, 56, 96, 116, 148, 152, 159–160
  grade ten, 25, 42, 56, 67, 125, 152
  grade twelve, 42, 56, 67, 79, 149, 152, 155–156
  multi-ethnic, 123

Hirschfeld, A., 28, 37, 38
Holland, J. V., 55, 64
Holman, C., vi, xxi, 41–54
Homes, single-parent, 65–78
Honesty, 155, 165, 166
Hope chest, activity, 12, 20, 31, 73, 134
Host/hostess, to new students, 58, 59
Howard, M. A., 159, 169
Huey, W. C., 142, 148
Human relations, 123–140, 141

I

I Got Rhythm, activity, 11
I learned statements, activity, 16–17, 99, 107–108, 128
I messages, communication, 10, 118
Icebreakers (*see* Activities, Energizers) 57, 68
Important person, activity, 26, 27
Incidents, ethnic-involved, 123
Interest inventories, 102
Interests, 96, 103, 104
    appraisal of, 105, 111–112
    definition, 101
Interventions, 115
Interview,
    screening, xviii, 4–5, 15, 25–26, 42–43,
    screening peer counselors, 143
Introductions, members', 55–62, 81
Isolation, 123

J

Jersild, A. T., 157, 169
Johnson, D. W., 126, 130
Jones, J. E., 126, 140
Jot list, writing a, 81
Journal,
    peer-counselors', 144, 146, 147
    test-taking, 44, 47
    writing entries in a, 91
Juniors, high school, 42, 56, 61, 67, 79, 95, 125
"Just Say No," groups, 150

K

Kaplan, D. M., 55, 64
Katahn, M., 42, 54
Kelly, J. M., 96–97, 114
Klima, M., 24, 38
Kranzow, G. W., 131, 140
Krumboltz, J. D., 124, 140
Krumboltz, H. B., 124, 140
Kumar, V., 158, 169

L

Lachance, L., 149, 150
Larsen, P., 157, 158, 159, 169
Leader's objectives, 24
Leader's procedures (*see* Group sessions)
Leader (*see* Group leader)
Learning, relevance, 95, 141
Learning style, determination of, 7–8, 18–19
Letter,
    notification to members, 31
    parent permission, 13–14, 43, 56
Leveling, activity, 23–24, 29
Levels, anxiety, 43–45
Life-plan, 96
Life-styles, 96, 98, 141, 153
Limits, 151
Listening skills (*see* Skills, listening) 11–12, 84, 88, 97, 118, 126, 130, 141, 142, 143
Listening, barriers to effective, 10
Loneliness,
    drug abusers', 151
    new students', 55–56
Lunch partner, 59, 61
Lunch period, 56, 146
Lunter, M., vi, xxi, 3–21

M

Magic box, activity, 10
Manni, J., 159, 169
Marriage, 158
Marshall, George C. High School, 141, 143
Mass. Inst. Tech. (MIT), 92
Materials, elementary school, 142, 145
McCann, B., vi, xxii, 115–122
McHolland, J. D., 105–107, 114

Meckstroth, E., 23, 38
Media, 103,
Meeting, parents', 67–68
Member letter, notification, 31,
Membership,
   heterogeneous, 96, 115, 117, 125
   referrals (*see* Group members, referrals) xviii, 4, 25, 42–43, 56, 67,
   selection (*see* Group members, selection)
   voluntary, xviii, 42, 56, 116, 125
Members, previous, 25, 117, 143, 151
Memory, dialogue with, 91
Metaphors, 131
Midpoint, feedback
Miller, D.C., 151, 156
Mini-Group, 116–117
Model,
   group counseling program, xix
   problem-solving, 17–18
   writing process, 89–90
Mohr, M. M., 79, 93
Moll, R., 82, 83, 93
Motivation, 81, 84, 85
Muia, J., 157, 168
Muro, J. J., 124
Murray, D., 79, 93
Myrick, R. D., 141, 148

N

Name Game, activity, 43, 58, 59, 60, 61, 62
Name Tag, activity, 5
Napier, R. W., 9, 20
National Honor Society, 57
Neighborhood effect, 117, 160
Network, 65
New student group, topics for, 63
New students, problems of, 55–64
Newsletters, 96, 116
Newspapers, 96, 116
Non-judgmental, 116, 152, 153, 154, 161
Norms, high school, 56
Norris, C., 158, 169
Norton, A., 65, 77
Notification,
   participants', 31,
   teachers', 14

O

Objectives,
   group leader's, 24, 68, 69, 70, 71, 72, 73,
   group session, 97, 98, 99, 100, 101, 102, 103
   members' personal, 26–31, 43–48, 68
Occupations, 99 (*see* Careers, Vocations)
Oetting, E. R., 151, 156
Organization, priority, 118
Orientation program, 142

P

Palmo, A., 159, 169
Parent advocacy, 67–68
Parent approval, 13–14, 25, 43
Parent invitation, 67, 97, 97–98
Parent involvement, 67
Parent letter,
   invitation, 67
   permission, 13–14, 43, 56, 68
Parent permission, letter, 13–14, 43, 56, 68
Parents,
   career guidance of, 97–98 (*see* Career, parents)
   concerns of, 95
   experience, 97–98, 104
   group session for, 81, 84, 97–98, 103–104
   influence, 95, 97
   meeting, 25, 67–68, 97–98
   personal contact, 25, 67, 160
   single, 65–66
   writing of, 80, 84
Participants, notice to, 31
Pass,
   guidance-hall, 57, 123
   opportunity to, 70, 97, 116, 131
Peer counselor, defined, 141
Peer counselors, 57, 58, 141–148
Peer influence, 150
Peer relationships, 55–56, 66
Peer tutors, 57
Peer, G. G., xiii, xiv
Peng, S. s., 158, 169
Perception, 152
Perfection bingo, introductions, 36
Perfectionism, gifted students', 23–39
Perfectionist, questionnaire, 34

Performance, academic, 3-21
Perlstein, R., vi, xxi, 79-93
Permission,
 parental, xix, 4, 13-14, 25, 56
 teacher, 25
Person, influential, 84, 86, 90-91, 163
Personal essays, 83
Personal goals (*see* Goals, individual
 personal)
 questionnaire, 16
Personal traits, questionnaire, 104
Perspectives, 95
Peters, L. J., 65, 77
Pfeiffer, J. W., 126, 140
Philadelphia, H.S., 158, 169
Philosophy, counseling, 152
Physical manifestations, stress, 42, 44,
Plan, group counseling (*see* Group sessions)
Plans,
 peer-counseling, 143
 post-secondary, 97, 105
Poem, Adam and Me, 28, 37
Poster, group-counseling, 13, 96, 135
Potential, individual, 115-122
Power, H. W., 93
Pre-examination, questionnaire, 46, 48,
 50-51
Pregnancy, 158, 159
Prejudice, 116, 125, 133, 134, 161
Prejudices, list of, 132, 139
Presentation, classroom, 25, 81-82
Pressure,
 academic, 118
 adolescent development, 55-56
Previous members, references of, 25
PRIDE, 149
Princeton University, 83
Priorities, setting, 118
Problems,
 prevention, 149
 students', xvii, 154
 substance-abuse, 149
Problem solving, 66, 72-73, 82, 115, 116, 125
 model for, 17-18
 steps in, 7, 17-18, 29
Procedures,
 group counseling (*see* Group sessions)
 leaders', 97-104
Procrastination, 79, 91

Progoff, I., 79, 93
Program,
 group-counseling, xvii-xix
 peer-counseling, 141-148
Progress reports, 3, 4
Project, peer-counseling, 141-148
Projective drawing, teenager, 71
Psychodramas, 125
Psychology, 142
Public address, 126
Publicity, groups (*see* Groups, publicity)
Publicize groups, poster to, 13,

Q

Qualifications, peer-counselors', 143
Questionnaire,
 ability appraisal, 102, 112-113
 About Me, 128, 134, 137-138
 anxiety scale, 45, 50
 aptitude, 102, 112
 autobiography, 113
 career planning, 104-113
 career settings, 110-111
 divorce, 74-75
 educational level, 109
 group evaluation, 16-17, 33, 37-38, 53-54,
  62-63, 76, 77, 89, 113-114, 122,
  139-140, 168
 group feedback, 33
 I Learned, 16-17, 107-108
 I Would Like . . . , 117, 120
 interests, 101, 111
 learning style, 18, 19
 perfectionism, 34
 personal drug-abuse, 153-154
 personal goals, 16
 personal traits, 98, 104
 pre-examination, 46, 48, 50-51
 school incidents, 8
 school subjects, 110
 study habits, 9,
 substance-abuse, 153-154
 test-taking, 53
 values, 105-107
 work, 108
 writing workshop, 89
Questions,
 college application, 91-92

Questions (*continued*)
  direct, 154
  drug-free interview, 153–154
  Getting to Know You, 135–136
  group counseling, 31–32, 117
  growth groups, 118
  open-ended, 118
Quiz, test-taking, 48, 53

R

Race relations, 123–140
Rank order, goals, 70
Ratliffe, S., 145, 148
Reading, 18
Recommendations,
  peer counselor, 143
  previous members', 151
Referrrals,
  group membership (*see* Group members, referral for)
  group membership, 67 (*see* Group members, referral)
Referral sources, groups (*see* Group members, referrals for)
Relationships, 66, 68, 118
Relaxation, 42
Relaxation exercises, 42, 46–47, 50
Report cards, 3
Requirements,
  academic, 57–61
  career, 100
Resources,
  career center, 103, 104
  peer counseling, 142, 145
  writing essays, 93
Respect, 118, 123, 153
Responsibility, group members, 155
Richards, A., 66, 69, 71, 77
Riddick, G. g., vi, xxii, 123–140
Ripple, G., 90, 91, 93
Risk taking, 82, 131, 152, 164
Rokeach, 17, 20
Role models, group, xviii, 4, 42, 57, 67, 125, 141, 160,
Role play, 125, 146
  communication skills, 10–12
Role reversal, 131
Roles in the family, identify, 72

Rose, S., 42, 54
Rotating schedule, group meetings, 14–15, 25, 43, 57, 96
Rules,
  facilitate communication, 118, 121, 126, 127
  group, 126, 161–163
  group, 5, 15–16, 43, 57, 58, 68, 96, 97
  school, 56

S

SADD, 150
Safety, physical, 124
Salovey, P., 142, 148
Sammons, M., 124, 125, 140
Saslaw, Eleanor, vi, vii, xxi, 23–39
Savitsky, A. J., 158, 169
Sawyer, A. P., 158, 169
Scale, anxiety, 46, 50
Schedule,
  group counseling, xviii–xix, 14–15 xviii–xix, 14–15, 96, 155
  personal daily, 9
  rotating, xviii–xix, 14–15, 25, 43, 57, 96, 125
  school, 142
School, dislike, 158, 159
School subjects, career related, 99, 110
Schools, elementary, 141, 142, 158
Schools, intermediate, 141, 142, 148, 160
Screening (*see* Group members, screening)
  individual, 15, 25–26, 42, 43, 67, 96, 117, 125, 152–154
  peer counselors', 143
Selection,
  group members (*see* Group members, selection)
Self-acceptance, 129
Self-awareness, 98
Self-centered, 151
Self-concept, 24, 164, 165
Self-confidence, 82, 142, 150, 159, 161, 167
Self-dignity, 150
Self-disclosure, 79
Self-discovery, 85, 88
Self-esteem, 133, 159
Self-exploration, 79, 83
Self-image, 116, 157
Self-inventory, 166
Self-knowledge, 81, 86

Self-respect, 150
Self-revelation, 162-163
Self-talk, negative to positive, 42, 67, 159, 165, 166
Self-understanding, 79-93
Self-worth, 82, 157, 159
Seminars, group counseling, 3-21, 23-39, 55-64, 65-78, 95-114, 152
Seniors, high school, 42, 56, 61, 67, 79, 95, 125, 152
Separation, pain of, 65,
Sessions,
    evaluation (*see* Groups, evaluation)
    evaluation of separate, 16-17, 33, 129, 130, 131
    evening, 96
    follow-up, 13, 134, 167
    parents', 81
    planned group, 5-13, 26-31, 43-49, 57-62, 68-73, 84-88, 97-104, 118, 126-135, 144-147
Sewell, T., 159, 169
Sheridan, J. T., 65, 66, 78
Shertzer, B., 157, 158, 159, 169
Sherwood, J. J., 126, 140
Shore, D., 83, 93
Similarities, members', 71-72
Simon, S. B., 19, 20, 145, 148
Single parent, 65, 66, 116
Sisk, D., 29, 30, 38
Skills,
    cognitive, 157
    counseling, 152, 154
    life, 96, 142, 157
    listening, 11-12, 84, 88, 97, 118, 126, 130, 141, 142, 143,
    responding, 143
    test-taking, 42,
Social dynamite, dropouts, 157
Social lives, previous drug-abusers', 149, 151
Social worker, school, 152
Society, changing, 95
Sophomores, high school, 25, 42, 56, 61, 67, 125
Sports program, 59-60
Statements, prejudicial, 133
Status, socio-economic, 158
Stereotypes, 66, 132, 134
Strenger, S., 42, 54

Strength bombardment, 62, 119, 129, 165
Stress,
    divorce, 65, 66
    family, 79
    gifted students', 24,
    new students', 55-56,
    physical manifestations, 42, 44
    reduction, 41-54, 116
    test-taking, 41
    writing, 79
Strother, J., 55, 56, 64
Structure, group, 119
Student leaders, 56, 59, 61
Student officers, 59, 61
Students,
    elementary school, 142
    eligible for group, 117
    English as a Second Language, 56 (*see* ESL)
    high-risk, 55, 157, 169
Study conditions, 9
Study habits, 4
Study skills, 6, 91
Substance-abuse, prevention of, 116, 149-156
Sugarman, D., 41, 54
Sunburst communications, 71, 78
Support,
    emotional group, 152, 154, 159, 160, 65, 67, 81, 142, 150, 151
Suspensions, school, 168
Swaim, R., 150, 156
Symptoms, substance-abuse, 149

T

Takai, R. T., 158, 169
Tasks, new students', 55-56
Teacher(s), xix, 4-5, 25, 42-43, 47, 56, 57, 155, 160
    acceptance of new students, 55-56
    notification, 14, 25, 96
    referrals from, 42, 143
Teenagers, 55, 65, 71
Tension, ethnic, 123, 131
Tension, family, 80
Termination, group, 73
Test anxiety, 41-58
Test-taking,
    conditions, 48

Test-taking (*continued*)
  feedback, 91
  journal, 44, 47
  quiz, 48
  skills, 42–43, 47–48
  tips, 47, 52
  writing about, 91
Testing time, 47, 52
Tests,
  differences, 41, 46, 47, 48
  preparation for, 43, 47, 52, 57, xix, 43,
The Gifted Kids' Survival, 23, 28, 39
Thinking, critical, 96
Thomas, C C, xv
Tindall, J., 141, 148
Tolan, S., 23, 38
Topics,
  growth groups, 118–119
  new student seminars, 63–64
Training, peer counselor, 142
Traits, personal, 98, 104–105
Transition, school-level, 142, 145
Treatment, substance-abuse, 149, 151, 153
Trotzer, J., 20, 21, 126, 131, 140
Truancy, 65
Trust, 80, 128, 131, 152, 161, 164
Tsui, A., 124, 125, 140
Tutors, peer, 57,

U

Unemployment, dropout, 157
Units, life, 98, 99
Univ. of Pa., 92
Use of test time, 47, 52,

V

Values, 141, 152, 159, 96, 97, 98, 105–107, 108, 125, 126

Values auction, 98, 105–107
Vietnamese, 125
Virginia Tech., xv
Vocabulary, feeling, 75–76, 129
Vocations, 99
Voice, writing, 80, 83, 84
Voluntary membership, xviii, 42, 56, 116, 125
Volunteers, 58, 99, 127, 129, 130, 131, 134, 166
Volz-Patton, R., 96–97, 114
Voss, H., 159, 169
VPI, xv

W

Way-out, activity, 7
Webb, J., 23, 38
Wells, H. C., 126, 140, 145, 148
Wendling, A., 159, 169
Wheeler, L., 158, 169
Wickendon, J. W., 83, 93
Willis, I., 66, 69, 71, 77
Winerip, M., 80, 93
Work ethic, 99, 108
Work, importance, 108, 158
Worksheets, 98, 104–105, 105–107, 108, 109, 110–111, 112–113
Workshops,
  family, 80, 81, 84
  introductory, 81, 84
World, changing, 141
Writer, reluctant, 79
Writing, 79–93
  examples, 84, 90–91
Writing activity, 83
Writing process, 89–90
Writing workshops, family, 80
  free, 79, 82, 85
  model for, 81–84, 88, 89–90